What is my Plant Telling Me?

WHAT IS MY PLANT TELLING ME?

AN ILLUSTRATED GUIDE TO HOUSEPLANTS
AND HOW TO KEEP THEM ALIVE

EMILY L. HAY HINSDALE
ILLUSTRATIONS BY LONI HARRIS

SIMON ELEMENT

NEW YORK   LONDON   TORONTO   SYDNEY   NEW DELHI

**SIMON
ELEMENT**

An Imprint of Simon & Schuster, Inc.
1230 Avenue of the Americas
New York, NY 10020

First Simon Element hardcover edition September 2022

SIMON ELEMENT is a trademark of Simon & Schuster, Inc.

For information about special discounts for bulk purchases, please contact Simon & Schuster Special Sales at 1-866-506-1949 or business@simonandschuster.com.

The Simon & Schuster Speakers Bureau can bring authors to your live event. For more information or to book an event, contact the Simon & Schuster Speakers Bureau at 1-866-248-3049 or visit our website at www.simonspeakers.com.

Interior design by Laura Levatino

Manufactured in China

10 9 8 7 6 5 4 3 2 1

Library of Congress Cataloging-in-Publication Data
Names: Hay Hinsdale, Emily L., author. | Harris, Loni, illustrator.
Title: What is my plant telling me? : an illustrated guide to houseplants and how to keep them from dying / by Emily Hinsdale, illustrated by Loni Harris.
Description: First Simon Element hardcover edition. | New York, NY : Simon Element, 2022.
Identifiers: LCCN 2021043099 (print) | LCCN 2021043100 (ebook) | ISBN 9781982189815 (hardcover) | ISBN 9781982189822 (ebook)
Subjects: LCSH: House plants. | Indoor gardening. | Handbooks and manuals.
Classification: LCC SB419 .H395 2021 (print) | LCC SB419 (ebook) | DDC 635.9/65–dc23
LC record available at https://lccn.loc.gov/2021043099
LC ebook record available at https://lccn.loc.gov/2021043100

ISBN 978-1-9821-8981-5
ISBN 978-1-9821-8982-2 (ebook)

For my roots: Mom, Dad, and Andy

Contents

Contents

WHAT IS MY PLANT TELLING ME?

Introduction

Remember that special day you brought home your new houseplant? Full of optimism and enthusiasm for your precious new member of the family, you showered it with love and plenty of water. You watched each new leaf unfurl, admired its glossy foliage or its brilliant blooms, posted daily plant reports on every social media platform you could find, and bragged to your friends about how your plant is the most remarkable plant of them all.

And then one day, you came home to find yellow leaves. Yellow leaves! What happened?! You gave this plant every possible advantage and here it is drooping around the house like it's not even trying.

What's a devoted plant parent to do?

Don't panic. And stop crying into your cactus; they don't like that much moisture anyway. Let's work the problem. Less pathos, more pothos.

The steps toward bringing your green buddy back to health are usually straightforward and doable. While your list of basic needs is extensive (pizza, coffee, Netflix, yoga pants, wine, chocolate, tacos, etc.), plant needs are simple: water, light, soil. Align those needs for your particular plant in your particular home and you two can grow together in harmony.

Fortunately for you, plants—unlike your ex—are good communicators. Most of the time, they will give out a few key signals when they're less than satisfied with your current relationship.

Don't speak plant? That's why we're here, ready to brush up your bromeliad, dust off your dracaena, and increase your fern fluency. Each type of plant will have specific signals for specific concerns, so it's important to study up on your own houseplant. However, there are a few introductory phrases that will help you establish a basis of communication to get started. Repeat after us: water, light, soil.

WATER

Like you, your plant is largely made up of water. Also like you, too little water will parch it and too much water will drown it.

Improper watering is at the root of most plant disasters. Underwatering deprives your plant of the wet stuff it so needs to keep from drying out. The soil will dehydrate, making it more difficult to get it to absorb moisture when you do finally water again. The plant will droop and brown. Overwatering, however, is the more frequent cause of plant disasters. Anxious plant parents will apply the H_2O aggressively and constantly until their poor plant is bogged down in a muddy mess of soil. Good for tadpoles, bad for plants. In all that wet, roots rot, spreading up into yellow leaves, soft and flabby stems, and eventually a dead plant.

A general rule of thumb for plant watering schedules—stick that thumb in the soil. Wet? Don't water. Damp? Excellent. Dry? Water, please.

When it is time to water, pour it on heavily enough for water to flow freely through the soil and out the drainage holes. This will ensure that your plant is wet, the soil is wet, and the excess water has washed away any soil or fertilizer impurities.

Knowing how frequently to water does depend on your type of plant. Some, like succulents and cacti, prefer to have their soil dry out completely before being watered again. Others, like ferns and figs, need to have their soil stay moist at all times.

Some plants—and some locations—will also need some attention to moisture in the air. Many indoor houseplants hail originally from tropical climes and are therefore used to steamy air and sultry breezes. This is easy to provide if you're houseplanting in Florida, less so if you hang out in Colorado. Misting the air around the plant can help but can be a bit of a chore, and some plants don't like wetness on their leaves. The reliable trick employed by serious indoor gardeners is also the easiest. Place a tray of pebbles under or near your plant. Get those pebbles wet—not sitting in a pool of water, just wet—and they will evaporate damper air around your plant.

For all plants, drainage is critical—a pot without holes in the bottom will unavoidably have a soggy bottom. If your pot overflows into a saucer, dump extra water out of the saucer for the same reason. If your teacup overflows into the saucer, surreptitiously dump the extra tea into a nearby houseplant. Manners.

LIGHT

All those useful labels pasted to plant pots at the plant store say things like "bright indirect light" or "low light." Say what?

Here's a general guide, though it may involve a lot of time sitting and staring at a window.

Low light:	less than 4 hours of sun
Medium light:	4 to 6 hours of sun
Bright light:	more than 6 hours of sun

Identify the light sources in your home. This means find the windows. Which direction do the windows face? Break out that compass (we bet there's one on your cell phone). South-facing windows get more intense light, or direct light. North-facing windows get less intense light, or indirect light. If the window is otherwise unobstructed, the light can still be "bright" while also being indirect. East- and west-facing windows tend to get medium light. What is medium light? you ask. Stand by your east/west windows. It's that. (It's indirect light.)

What kind of view do you enjoy? If you're looking out at shady trees (yay!) or the wall of another building (sigh), this window probably doesn't get a huge amount of bright sun. This means it's low light.

A couple of other light tips. Rotating your plant periodically will keep it evenly leaved and growing straight—the plant will lean into the sun. The brighter the light, the faster water will evaporate from the soil and from the plant itself, so keep in mind the quality of light while learning your watering routine.

Another routine to mind: dusting. This is more than tidying up; this is to help your plant breathe. As dust builds up on leaves, it blocks the sunlight, making it harder for your plant to photosynthesize. Photosynthesis is the plant's version of breathing—plants use sunlight to turn carbon dioxide (reminder: this is what you breathe out) into sugars that the plants use for energy, or food. If sunlight can't get through the layer of filth graying those leaves, your plant will not eat tonight. Smooth, flat-leaved plants can be gently wiped down with a damp cloth. Many-leaved or fronded plants will benefit from a shower to rinse away dust. And very delicate leaves that prefer to avoid getting wet, like those of an African violet, can be gently brushed off with a toothbrush.

Whatever light you have, you can still grow a plant! Just choose wisely.

SOIL

Let's talk dirty.

Most houseplants root in some form of soil. How your plant grows will decide which kind of soil you select for potting. A plant that wants to stay moist all of the time will need a rich, peaty, absorbent soil. A plant that likes to dry out wants a lighter, sandier soil. A plant that demands a little special treatment may persuade you to invest in a special potting mix, like an orchid mix.

Whatever soil type your plant demands, keep in mind that potting mixes exist for a reason. Digging up a scoop of dirt from your backyard will rarely suffice; potting mixes are created for the special circumstances and needs of an indoor plant. Added items, like perlite, will help soil drain faster in a pot. Beneficial nutrients that an outdoor plant might get from fallen leaves, decaying plant matter, and friendly worms are mixed into indoor plant soil.

Once you've picked the right soil, it's just as important to pick the right pot. A huge pot will leave your small plant with wet roots while it waits for all the moisture to evaporate. In a too small pot, the plant's roots will take up all the space, leaving little room for soil to absorb water and provide nutrients.

Some plants favor annual repotting into bigger pots as they grow. Others are happy where they are for years. But all of them will need a periodic soil refresh. Scoop out or replace old soil and add in some fresh stuff to keep your houseplant energized.

Unless, of course, you're raising an epiphyte, like an air plant or other soil-free indoor plant. You could have skipped reading this section.

In each plant profile in this book, you will find a frightening list of things that can go wrong. Spider mites! What are those? Fungus? Overfertilizing? Like a parenting book listing a million potential childhood diseases, this can be overwhelming. Remember, most of the time, you can thwart small problems with small adjustments. And a plant that is generally healthy generally avoids the bigger problems of pests and fungus.

So don't worry, relax, and take a deep breath of that clean, detoxified, oxygenated air that a good houseplant contributes to your atmosphere.

African Violet

Saintpaulia Ionantha

Light:	bright indirect sunlight
Water:	water when dry and drain well
Soil:	peaty soilless mix (*not* violet mix)
Food:	fertilize weekly
Pot:	underpot; repot annually

Though modest as any violet should be, the African violet still has plenty to say for itself. So much to say, in fact, that it has developed what could be described as a cult following, with entire greenhouses and plant businesses dedicated to producing an increasing variety of colors and sizes.

We love the African violet for its flowers, an array of vivid purples and pinks and blues, so rare in the stolidly green world of houseplants. One can picture that dramatic color catching the eye of German colonial baron Walter von Saint Paul-Illaire (hence

1

its Latin name, *Saintpaulia*), who plucked it from its Tanzanian home and dispatched its seeds to Europe in 1892, launching it into houseplant fame.

Okay, maybe you weren't picturing that when you spotted an adorable velvet-leaved, mauve-flowered plant in the grocery story. But if you are going to raise this still eye-catching staple of the houseplant world, you must be willing to acknowledge its heritage. It is African, and though an endangered species in the wild, from your windowsill it still dreams of its warm homeland in rainforested mountains.

Your job is to re-create that tropical environment to keep your African violet comfortable. Light, and lots of it, but not direct sun; the rays should filter through to your plant as though through tall rainforest trees. It prefers soil that is peaty and light, draining quickly. (You may spot soil labeled "violet mix" in the gardening store—don't be tempted. "African" violets are quite different in their origins and needs from the Northern Hemisphere species beloved of Sappho.) Offer it warm, humid air and plenty of nutrients from regular fertilizing, to imitate the wealth of nutrients in forest floor detritus.

Proper watering technique, however, is the real secret weapon in African violet care. Fail to water the right way and it may break out in spots—literally!

Yellow spots on the leaves means your watering has been too splashy. When cold water hits one of those fuzzy leaves, the shock causes leaf cells to collapse, leaving you with a plant with the pox. Keep this in mind when you're dusting, too; this isn't a plant you can shower down to dust. Brush dusty leaves off with a toothbrush!

Watering the right way can be easy enough if approached with patience and forethought. Let's review some rules:

- Use warm or room-temperature water. It's best to let the water sit out overnight so it can come to room temperature and let the chlorine and fluoride included in our tap water (safe for us but icky for plants) evaporate.

- Don't splash it about; water carefully! Gently hold leaves out of the way, and invest in a watering can with a narrow spout.
- While some choose to water from the bottom or poke the waterspout into soil to avoid the leaves, it's best to make sure the water is draining all the way through the roots and soil. Flowing water rinses away salts and other impurities and makes sure all the roots get a drink. Carefully pour water in at the plant's base until water flows from drainage holes.
- Drain well! This houseplant won't tolerate pooling water in the bottom of the pot. Make sure that your pot has a drainage hole and that you immediately empty any water that collects in its saucer.
- Just because this is a rainforest native doesn't mean it accepts constant rain. The soil should be dry to the touch before you water again. When in doubt, water less, not more.

Anytime your African violet seems less than its full, flowering self, ask yourself first if you've been following the watering rules. Only then can we take a look at a few other culprits in violet unhappiness:

Dry, cold air. Yellow leaves? Few flowers? Rotting stem? What goes for water temperature goes for temperature in general for the African violet setting. It likes to be comfortable. If you find the ambient temperature pleasant, so will the African violet. If you're wearing two sweaters and a hat indoors, warm it up! And add a little evaporation humidity by setting your plant on a tray of wet pebbles.

Too much sun. Yellow leaves are again what to watch for. African violets are shade plants, so avoid hot, bright windowsills.

Too little sun. When it stops producing blooms, lead it to the light. Especially during winter months, make sure your tropical friend gets ten to fourteen hours of light—some fanatics even use fluorescent grow lights.

Suckers. These are baby plants popping up along the plant's base, sucking nutrients from the parent plant. They've got to go. Cut them away with a sharp, clean knife.

Scraggly growth. Time to repot! And fertilize. Don't be surprised if your plant goes into a fit of the sulks and refuses to bloom for a while after repotting. It will get over it.

Pests. Aphids or mites or whatever creepy-crawlies are causing yellow leaves and limp leaves on your African violet should be removed right away. Prune affected leaves and treat with insecticide.

Now that you are fully conversant with the needs of African violets, how about going for another round? Time to propagate! Remember that most African violets sold in stores are hybrids. If you harvest its seeds for new plants, you never know what kind or color you might get. If you want a clone of your original plant, root it directly from one of its leaves for a small but exact match.

AIR PLANTS

TILLANDSIA

Light: bright indirect light
Water: weekly soak with careful drying
Soil: none!
Food: fertilize monthly, low-nitrogen mix
Pot: none!

Air plants are the modish darlings of today's interior designers with an eye for a look that's spare but with flair. These are not your average houseplants, settling their ample root bases in a hefty pot. Air plants instead literally thrive on air, perched wherever you feel like—pinned on a wall, scattered among shells or other knickknacks, or hanging from the chandelier. They thrive on air, light, and water, feeding themselves on photosynthesis alone. One has to admire their self-sustainability, but one also has to care for them properly. They might be unusual-looking, but they are still living beings.

Care is relatively straightforward. Make sure they get enough light, since they depend on plenty of light for photosynthesis. Water weekly with a good dunk in the sink, but let them dry completely before returning them to their perches. Once a month, add some water-soluble fertilizer to their bath. The more humid their location, the better, but they do need good air circulation. Tillandsia look oddly plastic, but they're not—enclosed terrariums are not the best option.

When your tillandsia's attitude turns less than airy, sorting through its worries starts with one simple question of identity: Is your air plant mesic or xeric? Getting away from dichotomous labels may be a good direction for humanity, but it's kind of necessary when you're having a heart-to-heart with a tillandsia.

- **Xeric *Tillandsia*** are covered with trichomes, tiny cups that capture moisture from the air and give the plant a silvery sheen. These plants are natives of arid climates, ready to handle low moisture and brighter sunlight.
- **Mesic *Tillandsia*** have a greener hue, fitting in with their rainforest origins. They are more accustomed to humid climates and indirect light.

With these differences in mind, a good way to head off future problems for your air plant is to make sure you select one that aligns with *your* natural habitat. Arizona readers might like a xeric companion, while those living in Florida humidity might want to opt for a mesic air plant. You can, however, adjust your own indoor environment to please your plant—just be prepared to meet needs that your home may not naturally include.

Too much water. A plant that is falling apart or soft in the center is probably suffering from rot, which starts when water collects between the leaves. If the rot appears as small brown patches on the outer leaves, gently remove them. If it's advanced to the point where leaves are falling off, it may be too late to save this one. Make sure to shake water off the leaves and let air plants dry out before returning them to their decorative spot.

Too little water. Dry and brown leaf tips can mean your air plant is getting dehydrated. Check the leaves—are they curving inward in a concave shape? Time for a soak and a reconsideration of how often you're watering. If this is a mesic variety, especially, keeping it in a humid location (like a bathroom) or misting between soaks can help keep it fresh.

Browning tips can also be a sign of stress. If your plant has recently been relocated or otherwise challenged, just keep treating it with care and it will likely improve on its own. Sometimes misting it between waterings can help.

A sad, wilted-looking air plant might just need better air circulation. It feeds on air—give it a constant fresh supply. Enclosed terrariums and vases won't work. If you can comfortably breathe in a space, so can your air plant.

Yellow leaves are your plant's way of saying they have had too much water and too much light! Stretch out time between waterings and keep your tillandsia out of direct rays.

Similarly, **brown spots on the leaves** might just be a sunburn! Air plants, even sun-happy xeric air plants, prefer indirect bright light. Move them out of direct rays and make sure they don't have water sitting on their leaves. Brown spots can also mean your tillandsia is overfertilized or could even be an early sign of fungus and mold. Treat it with a fungicide as soon as possible before it spreads deeper into the plant.

A common question from new air plant owners is: **What's this white stuff all over the leaves?** That's probably trichomes, the silvery, almost hairy-looking, minuscule cups all over air plant leaves (especially the xeric variety) that retain moisture from the air. They are a good thing!

My air plant just had a pup—now what? Aw, it's adorable. A tiny tintype of your beloved air plant. But why does the parent plant look like it's withering away? Some (though not all) tillandsia do die after producing a pup. Don't worry about it. It's the nature of things.

The list of air plant varieties available to add to your home decor is extensive, ranging from typical types available in any plant store to rare and protected species available only through specially licensed importers. Pick one for its look, but also make sure you are picking one that fits the environment you live in and level of care you are able to provide.

Aloe Vera

ALOE BARBADENSIS

Light:	bright indirect light
Water:	water when soil is dry, drain well
Soil:	cactus or succulent soil
Food:	fertilize at most annually
Pot:	wide, shallow pot

The celebrity of the *Aloe* genus, aloe vera is an easy-to-grow succulent more popular for its reputed healing powers than for its cuddliness. Its look is sculptural and austere, different from the leafy green style of vines or ferns. This houseplant is barbed and uncomfortable to encounter unawares. However, give it its own space and room for attitude and it can be a helpful and unique home addition without stressing you out over too many problems.

Aloe vera grows wild only in the mountains of Oman on the Arabian Peninsula, but it has been bred in homes and in temperate and tropical gardens for centuries. (Fun fact: While its Latin name comes from its reported origin in Barbados, it was actually imported to those islands by the Spanish.) It's not hard to obtain or maintain.

As with most succulents, nonintervention is the best way to ensure your plant's health. Water it only when the soil is dry, and make sure it's contained in a fast-draining soil in a fast-draining pot. Give it good access to light. If you are good to your aloe vera, it can live for many years, growing as high as three feet in the right conditions. When mature—and this may take as long for an aloe vera as it does for a human male—it can produce a spiky, brightly colored flower atop a long stalk. As it matures, it will also produce pups, or baby aloe vera plants growing around its base. When these pups have a few leaves of their own, they are ready for harvesting—pull or cut them away from the parent plant, let them dry for a day or two, and then plant them in their own new pot, watering well initially. The parent plant will grow stronger when the pups are removed, and you'll have a whole new set of aloe veras to enjoy.

To keep your aloe vera happy, watch for:

Rotting. This is the most common problem for an aloe vera. If you spot brown mushy splotches or entire leaves turning brown and soft, that's rot. This plant is getting too much moisture. Ease off the watering and wait until the soil is dry before watering more. Make sure the roots are not resting in water. A pot that doesn't drain or is too big for the root ball will allow water to collect around the roots, rotting it from the roots up. Dense, moist potting soil can also retain too much water for an aloe vera; use a lightweight cactus or succulent mix instead. If your aloe plant is brown and mushy at the center of its rosette leaf growth pattern, it may be too late to save. If you're just seeing a few brown leaves or patches, change your watering habits and pay attention to its sharp, serrated edges saying, "Back off."

Wilting. When we say dry soil, we don't mean desert sands drifting in the wind. A succulent retains moisture in its leaves, but it still needs water. If your aloe vera's leaves start to pucker, losing that plump succulent look, water it!

Bent or pale leaves. Let there be light! Aloe vera needs sunlight. While it can't tolerate direct rays, you still need to make sure this houseplant is getting at least six hours of bright light every day. When it's not getting enough light, the leaves can lose their bright green color and grow long and leggy, sometimes wrinkling or folding.

Orange or brown leaves. On the other hand, giving your aloe vera too much light can also cause problems. It may be known for its sunburn-soothing leaf gel, but aloe vera is a sunburn sufferer as well. Hot direct sun will toast those leaves, turning it from green to orange or brown. Move it off the windowsill to a spot that is well lit, but not a sunbath.

Yellow leaves or brown spots. Moving can be stressful. Your houseplant doesn't enjoy it any more than you do. If it has spent its early life on a store shelf, underwatered, overwatered, or moved around, it can struggle. Get it on a watering schedule in a stable location, and it will usually adjust and green up again.

As much as you are trying to get to know your aloe vera's needs, it is far less interested in serving yours. We know you can find social media posts about it as a cure for everything from a sunburn to digestive health issues, but seriously, this stuff is not magic. Proceed with caution: Large enough doses of aloe vera can result in allergies, toxicity causing, um, laxative effects, and even heart and kidney failure. But as long as you are not allergic to it, you can harvest the gel from its leaves as a skin ointment. Cut a leaf off near the base and break it open to squeeze out the gel. It can soothe (but not heal) minor burns.

Areca Palm

Dypsis lutescens

Light: bright indirect light

Water: moist soil, water weekly

Soil: peaty with perlite for good drainage

Food: fertilize every two months

Pot: snug fit, good drainage

Adding grace and elegance to any setting, the areca palm is popular in tropical outdoor gardening, but also works well as an indoor large-sized houseplant; if raised in a loving home, it can reach well over six feet indoors! Its tall, slender stalks are reminiscent of a clump of bamboo, but its fronds splay out into rustling, feathery green displays.

Like many palms, it's of tropical origin and will need to be handled accordingly. Humidity, moisture, and bright light are necessities, not just interests. Areca palm is not a plant for a beginner; it takes some care and attention, which may be part of what put it on the list of threatened plants in the wild. If you want an easy palm, take a look at a parlor palm or kentia palm. If you are sure you want the challenging areca, be prepared to pay attention and be a good listener when it communicates its finicky needs.

Is your areca palm troubled? At the first hint of dissatisfaction, its leaf tips turn brown. They turn brown in response to a myriad of perceived and real neglect. You will need to be a bit of a detective to sort through this list of concerns to identify the culprit.

Brown tips mean:

Too wet. Start with a pot or container that drains well and use a peaty soil with plenty of perlite mixed in to promote good drainage. Boggy soil will rot roots fast, and mushy roots can't absorb the water or nutrients the plant needs. Check that the top two inches of soil are slightly dry before watering again, and when you do water, make sure it drains completely.

Too dry. Tropical plant means moist soil. The soil should never entirely dry out, but always retain a little moisture—again, that's moist, not soaked.

Wrong water. The fluoride and chlorine added to our municipal water supply have done amazing things for halting bacterial spread for humans, but the areca palm is unimpressed. Use distilled water, or for a cheaper and easier choice let water sit out for twenty-four hours to evaporate chemicals before feeding to your palm.

Not enough light. These palms need a lot of light. Choose a cheery corner near an east- or west-facing window for reliable sunshine.

But not direct light. Many hours of intense direct sun rays will burn the leaves.

Proper fertilizer. It likes to eat consistently, so fertilize every two months. Make sure to rinse the fertilizer through the soil with a good watering subsequently to prevent fertilizer buildup, which can cause—you guessed it—brown leaf tips.

Not enough humidity. Areca palms will protest any dryness, so keep yours away from AC vents, heaters, and very hot or very cold windows. If your air is particularly dry, place a tray of wet pebbles under or near your palm. Grouping it with other plants can also help raise the ambient humidity to a comfortable level.

Repotting. Just don't. The areca palm liked where it was before. It prefers a snug-fitting container, keeping its roots cramped. It finds being repotted stressful, so stick to refreshing its soil periodically rather than changing its home.

Pests. While not particularly prone to pests, there are still some indoor annoyers that can show up, such as whiteflies, mealybugs, aphids, scale, or mites. Treat with neem oil as soon as possible.

Pruning. You may be tempted to cut away the brown-tipped leaves. Remember, the plant is still using the green part of the leaf for photosynthesis, so removing it can cause additional stress and more brown tips! If you're really bothered by the brown tips, you can carefully trim just the tips with clean scissors. Or you could just find something more interesting to worry about.

If you have made your way through this exhaustive and exhausting checklist of areca palm problems and helped your palm perk up, full marks for patience. Your reward is many years of this gold-stalked, green-leafed beauty bringing tropical paradise into your home.

BASIL

OCIMUM BASILICUM

Light: full sun
Water: frequently, when leaves start to droop
Soil: rich, light soil
Food: weak weekly fertilizer
Pot: good drainage

It's fast-growing and productive, bushy and bright green, aromatic and delicious. Who wouldn't want to make basil the centerpiece of their windowsill herb garden? Basil is a staple in many cuisines around the world, with a dazzling array of varieties to tempt your taste buds and your green thumb. Whether your herb garden starts with seedlings or from seed, this is a houseplant that will quickly make you feel like a gardening success.

Until it doesn't, because all of a sudden your beautiful bush of basil has gotten woody and scraggly, with sharp-tasting leaves diminishing into a spur of small purple flowers. It's okay! You have not failed to care for your basil. Some houseplants are perennial, growing with you year after year. Basil, on the other hand, is an annual, which means it lasts for a brief season before you need to start over with a new plant. Accept this life cycle, since you can't change it. Maybe even use it as an opportunity to try a different variety of the plant with your next effort. Sweet basil? Thai basil? Opal basil? Try them all!

Though each basil plant will not last *your* lifetime, that doesn't mean you should ignore the problems that might prevent it from living life to the fullest.

Finding the right location for growing basil is half the battle. You don't need a large container or a sizable garden; a good-sized crop of basil will be happy in a small pot on your windowsill. That windowsill, however, is worth noting. This is not a plant that grows well in low light or dark corners. It will turn brown or grow small, misshapen leaves when away from the window. Basil needs lots of direct sun, as much as six to eight hours a day. Select a spot where the light floods in and your basil will flourish.

Now that your basil is well positioned to grow, here are some other issues to watch for:

Underwatering and overwatering. Underwatering is easy to spot—the leaves start to droop and look limp, even shriveling if left parched too long. Water well, drain thoroughly, and your basil should perk right up. Overwatering is a more serious problem. If the leaves are yellowing and wilted in spite of recent watering, the soil may be too soaked around the roots to survive. Set the plant in the sun to dry out and hold off on watering for a while. If the roots have started to rot in the sodden earth, it may be too late for this basil plant. Next time, water only when it's starting to droop and make sure your pot has the opportunity to drain well. Your goal is damp soil, not wet.

Downy mildew. Basil is susceptible to several diseases and pests, the most common being downy mildew, a kind of fungus that thrives on humid conditions. Brown or white blemishes on the leaves as though they have gotten dirty around the edges? Look closely and you may be able to spot the downy, gray mildew growth that is slowly killing off the leaves. Prevent it by preventing conditions for mildew growth to begin with. Basil needs low humidity. Keeping it in a damp spot (next to a drafty window? in a bathroom?) won't work, nor will crowding it round with other plants. Basil needs good airflow and good dry space to flourish.

Black or brown stems. Fungi can also affect the stems, appearing as darker patches on the usually bright green stems and gradually spreading up the plant, yellowing leaves and killing the roots. There is not much you can do to save basil once this fungus has appeared except toss it fast so that it doesn't move on to additional plants.

Pests. Aphids. Thrips. Slugs. Basil is a popular snack for the insect world as well. If you spot tiny black or white spots on the leaves, holes spotting the leaves, or anything crawling around, break out the insecticide and hold off on harvesting for a while. Treat it early—once the bugs get hooked, it can be hard to get rid of them without getting rid of the whole plant.

Harvest your basil by snipping off an inch or two of basil leaf at a time with clean scissors. Pruning like this not only improves your spaghetti sauce but also extends the plant's life. The longer you can keep it trimmed back and not let it flower, the longer it will keep producing pesto. Bon appétit!

Begonia

Light: bright indirect sunlight

Water: water when soil surface is dry

Soil: peaty, well-draining soil

Food: diluted solution, monthly

Pot: repot rarely; refresh soil annually

It would take us most of this page to list all the types of begonias. There are thousands of begonia species and thousands more hybrids. Even commonly found species have numerous varieties, and your selection can come down to a matter of taste. Do you like them for their flowers? Do you like them for their leaves? Green leaves? Red leaves? White flowers? Pink flowers?

One thing you probably love about begonias is how quickly one little plant can turn into a forest of foliage for your houseplant collection. They breed like rabbits—pin one small leaf into some peaty soil or float a stem in a vase and you've got yourself a new begonia. This is a very cheap way to turn your home into a garden.

However, first you have to sort through the plethora of begonia options to identify the ideal plant to launch your begonia breeding colony. There are so many varieties to choose from—some better suited for indoor life than others—that enthusiasts have attempted to group them to differentiate. As most of these groupings have very little taxonomic or genetic reference, however, more helpful to the prospective begonia plant parent are these three questions:

1. **What's your style?** If you're looking for lush, interesting green or patterned foliage, stick with a foliage begonia, like the rex begonia. If you're looking to add color and a somewhat old-fashioned elegance to your home, there are several begonias that flower beautifully indoors, like the wax begonia.

2. **What's your locale?** In general, begonias like a tropical vibe: moist soil, humid air, and sunshine. Some begonias favor indirect light and more humidity. Others are up for full sun and drier air.

3. **What's your capacity and commitment level?** Stick an average garden-store wax begonia in some soil, water occasionally, and you're all set. But if you covet the ruffled brilliance of a tuberous begonia, prepare for patience, humidity, and light.

Now that you've selected your ideal begonia, let's get it set to grow well. Drainage is really important for these houseplants. Because their root systems tend to be shallow, a big, waterlogged pot will very quickly rot roots. Water when the surface of the soil is dry and avoid splashing the leaves, which can promote fungus growth. While flowering begonias need more humidity, all begonias need good airflow, so a closed container won't be an effective begonia home. Keep light indirect, but generally flowering plants need more light than foliage plants.

While the begonia varieties may not always agree with one another's sense of style, they do tend to see eye to eye (tuber to tuber?) on complaints.

Pruning. Showing a little leg is not a good thing in a begonia. Unimpeded, its stems will grow longer and longer. It may still flower and produce leaves on top, but the lower stem is left naked and scraggly. Periodically pinch back flowers and leaf clusters to encourage a bushier growth. Begonia foliage enthusiasts sometimes pinch off the unremarkable flowers to urge the gloriously patterned leaves to grow instead. Similarly, get rid of any dead or brown leaves right away. They aren't pretty and just serve as breeding grounds for fungus.

Watering care. Check the top inch of soil. Still wet? Don't water. Getting dry? Add water. Err on the side of dryness, even waiting until those juicy leaves look a little woebegone. *How* you water can be just as important as *when* you water. Water thoroughly, until water is running out of the drainage holes, and make sure all of the water has drained out. Standing water (puddling around the roots or the stem) causes rot. The roots will begin to turn mushy and die, the stem will soften and bend, and leaves will fall off. It's also wise to avoid splashiness or misting—water sitting on begonia leaves invites fungal infections.

Light side. Begonias will let you know if they've had too much (or not enough) light. Dry brown patches on the leaves? That's a begonia sunburn— get it out of the direct rays. Little flowering or less leaf patterning? A little more light, please! Leaning anxiously toward a window as it grows? Rotate! Make sure all sides get a moment in the sun.

Powdery mildew. We warned you about fungus! Powdery mildew is the most common begonia pest. It appears as white powdery patches on the leaves or causes distorted and spotted leaf growth; look closely and you may see threadlike growths in the white spots. Powdery mildew can spread quickly among the plants in your begonia collection (as well as to other houseplants), so treat it quickly. Isolate the sick begonia from other plants and remove its infected leaves. Treating the surrounding unaffected leaves with neem oil can help prevent its spread.

Mealybugs. While such infestations are not typical indoors, begonias can occasionally attract mealybugs—tiny gray clusters of bugs crawling along stems, sucking out your plant's juices like teeny-tiny vampires. Dab those bugs with a cotton swab or cotton ball dipped in rubbing alcohol, and that should eradicate the little monsters.

The challenges begonias pose are quickly mastered, so feel free to devote more of your time to gathering new types to add to your collection. And whether you've succumbed to the current craze for sophisticated foliage begonias or prefer the ruffled charms of a colorful tuberous begonia flower, be sure to take a moment to appreciate their fabulous names—'Stained Glass', 'Cracklin' Rosie', 'Regal Minuet'—not to mention the red-flowering species that serves as North Korea's emblematic flower, the Kimjongilia!

BROMELIAD

BROMELIACEAE

Light: bright indirect sunlight
Water: water when dry and drain well
Soil: fast-draining or orchid mix
Food: fertilize when flowering
Pot: fast-draining, on the small side

Beloved as a user-friendly, low-maintenance houseplant with a wild, colorful look year-round, bromeliads are a great starter option for the indoor gardening newbie. You can do this! Bromeliads can take some neglect and are relatively clear communicators. The more common species are easy to find and adapt well to indoor life.

You'll usually find bromeliads sold in soil-filled pots. But really, they need very little soil, and many don't even need a pot! They are usually epiphytic, meaning that in their natural setting they will grow attached to another species of plants, like a tree. They gather nutrients from the air, sun, and water, not from the soil or host plant. This makes potting a bromeliad the trickiest part of bromeliad parenthood. With a minimal root system, they won't cling to soil. Most species will want a fast-draining soil mix in a fast-draining pot. Some experts even recommend settling your bromeliad in an orchid soil mix. Or even without soil, as you would with its air plant relatives!

How to properly water a bromeliad is a topic of passionate debate for bromeliad buffs. Some promote adding water to the "cup" formed by encircling leaves at the center of the plant. This is its water catchment device in nature, providing a reliable water source with or without consistent rain. However, many argue that for the indoor plant fed on tap water, that cup fills up with salts and sometimes pests. If you do use the cup-fed method, be sure to rinse the cup out well monthly and consider using distilled water. Or just water the soil when it gets nice and dry. That seems like less work.

One oft-reported bromeliad "problem" stems from a confusion between flowers and leaves. That brightly colored cockscomb at the top of your plant—what is that? Even a Google search may give you the wrong answer. Some species of bromeliads (like the popular *Guzmania*) feature colored leaves, or bracts, of red, pink, yellow, or orange near the center of the plant. These are not flowers, and you can expect them to stay this color year-round. When a bromeliad does flower, it's hard to miss. The flower is dramatic, flamboyant, vividly colored, and usually rather oddly shaped. No dainty rosettes here. This is a stalk of pink and purple shoots or a stalk of flat red or yellow swords. That flower stalk is a long-term reward—they can last as long as three to six months—but when it turns brown and withers, don't worry! You haven't done anything wrong as a plant parent. Snip off the offending stalk and give your bromeliad a little fertilizer to rejuvenate.

Except that it may not rejuvenate. This is the other major concern bromeliad owners face: a bromeliad that dies after flowering. While you may miss your bromeliad friend, you need to accept that this is its life cycle. Many species (though not all!) die after flowering—but not before reproducing! Check the base of your dying bromeliad.

Do you see a much smaller version of it popping out alongside its roots? That's a pup, a baby bromeliad. When it's about a third of the size of the original plant, gently separate it from its parent and repot. It may be small, but it will get bigger and your bromeliad's life can continue.

However, brown stalks and leaves are not always a sign of a healthy life cycle. Here are a few things your bromeliad would like you to correct right away:

Yellow leaves or brown leaf tips. Remember when we said indirect light? Yellow leaves are a bromeliad sunburn. Get it out of the direct sun.

Dark green leaves. If your bromeliad started with a vivid chartreuse-green leaf or a variegated pattern but now has plain dark green leaves, it's not getting enough light. Move it to a brighter space.

Brown leaves. If you spot brown and even rotting leaves near the plant's base, you are probably keeping it too wet. Let that soil dry out a little and make sure it drains well. Collecting water and damp soil can rot the roots.

Pests. Aphids or mealybugs aren't too common with bromeliads, but if you see stippling on the leaves or see those little suckers crawling around, wipe them off with a cotton ball dipped in alcohol.

Bromeliads vary widely. Genuses like *Guzmania, Vriesea,* and *Cryptanthus* are among the more commonly available, but there are thousands of different types out there. Go wild. Your bromeliad certainly will.

pale, wrinkled leaves = not enough water

browning/rotting leaves + stems = too much water

Burro's Tail

Sedum morganianum

Light: bright indirect sunlight
Water: water when very dry, monthly
Soil: cactus soil, fast-draining
Food: rarely, use a diluted cactus fertilizer
Pot: don't repot!

How would you like to be named after what hangs from the hindquarters of a donkey? Perhaps this is why the burro's tail, or donkey's tail, is so finicky. Sure, it has the easy-to-please attitude of most succulents, but its touchy decision to discard its leaves at the slightest bump makes it a companion to keep an eye (but not a finger) on.

And how could you resist keeping an eye on a burro's tail? Despite its unattractive misnomer, this luxuriant succulent is sure to be the centerpiece of any houseplant or

brown spots on
leaves = fungus

yellow leaves =
too much sunlight

succulent collection. With its plump droplet-shaped leaves cascading in brilliant green tightly knit rows down a trailing stem, burro's tail is a showstopper in a hanging basket or on a high shelf.

Growing tips match those of most succulents. Burro's tail needs around six hours of good light—even sustained indoor artificial light will work—but not direct sunshine. Pot in a container that drains well and use cactus soil or an alternative that will drain quickly without retaining too much water along the way. Watering isn't something you'll have to worry about often—burro's tail likes to dry out between showers. In all but the driest climates, you may not need to water more than once a month! A little neglect doesn't hurt this little donkey.

Neglect should actually be your goal with a burro's tail. It drops its beady leaves easily, at the slightest jostle. If you need to be touchy-feely with your houseplants, you may want to select another option. When it does drop its leaves, ask yourself:

Have you bumped it or its pot?

Have you repotted it?

Have you moved it from room to room?

If your answer to any of these questions is yes, then your burro's tail is being clear with you: "Hands off." Otherwise, keeping a handle on this houseplant's needs is straightforward.

Browning or rotting leaves or stem: Too much wet stuff. Be sure to let the soil dry out completely between waterings, and make sure the water doesn't collect in the pot. Wet roots mean root rot for a succulent.

Pale or wrinkled leaves: Okay, you took the neglect too far. This plant needs water. Get that soil thoroughly wet and your dried-out burro's tail should recover quickly. If you leave it too long, this is yet another occasion in which leaves will start to fall off.

Yellow leaves: Some experts note that those vivid green leaves start to yellow when they get too much intense light. Keep it indirect.

Waxy substance on leaves: This is nothing to worry about. This is a natural substance the burro's tail produces to help retain more moisture in those succulent little green leaves. The substance rubs off when you touch it but will reemerge.

Brown spots on leaves: This could be a fungus. Move it away from other plants and check that it's not too moist. You can also treat the fungus with neem oil—although it will probably drop some leaves when you do!

By now you have tied your hands behind your back and are nervously avoiding even casual contact with your burro's tail. But there's an upside to its leaf shedding habits—that's how it propagates! Rescue those discarded green droplets (or pluck a fresh one from the plant) and place them in a pot of moist cactus soil. Keep that soil slightly damp with regular misting and you will soon see a brand-new burro's tail springing forth.

Cactus

Cactaceae

Light: bright indirect sunlight

Water: water when very dry, monthly

Soil: cactus soil, fast-draining

Food: cactus fertilizer, biweekly during spring/summer months

Pot: underpot with good drainage

The cactus only looks prickly. Once you get to know it, it's actually pretty easy to get along with. With a chill watering schedule and a minimal list of complaints, a cactus garden can be one of the more manageable indoor gardening endeavors.

When most people think *cactus*, they think of sharp spines. What they should think about is holes. Success at growing cacti depends on a pot with holes in the bottom to ensure that water drains out thoroughly. A jar or container without any drainage will just create muddy muck around the roots. A pot that's way too big for a little cactus will retain way too much water around the roots. Select one that fits your cactus snugly, and don't rush to repot every year. The choice of soil matters, too. Use a cactus soil or a mix that contains lots of perlite. Your goal here is for water to get the soil wet and then flow on through. Check out the cactus's native turf: desert. This isn't a place known for its pools of water, so banish that mirage from your cactus's home life as well. Water monthly, or when the soil is dry to the point of feeling sandy. Give it a thorough wetting at that time—no light sprinkles—until the water runs through the drainage holes. Then it's on its own for another month! As with most succulents, it likes around six hours of good light, but not direct rays (which have a tendency to turn even the greenest cactus yellow).

Most problems cactus growers experience stem from water problems. Cacti are so water-wary that they've largely given up the leafy look, opting instead for a predator-discouraging, water-loss-reducing, spiny aspect. They store fluid in their juicy succulent centers. Wet on the inside is fine; when they're getting too wet from the outside, those central stems and barrels are exactly where to watch for signs of rot.

Six signs of a cactus in a decline:

- **Shaky.** If your cactus jiggles or shifts around when you move it, its roots may be starting to rot, keeping it from clinging securely to the soil.
- **Brown or black.** If you see brown or black patches, that part of the cactus is dying.
- **Smelly.** If your cactus pot is starting to smell like a garbage can, something is rotten in the state of Denmark.
- **Mushy.** The mushy parts are rotten. A cactus should never be mushy.
- **Leaky.** If fluid is leaking out of the cactus, there's a rotten spot inside.

What should you do if you identify any of these symptoms? Cactus doctor to the rescue! If it is possible to excise the rotten tissue, cut it out. Then the spot can scab over and the plant can keep growing. If you suspect root rot, remove the cactus from its soil (try wrapping it in paper to protect your hands from spines) and check the roots. Cut away brown ones (these are rotten) and keep any white ones—these are still viable. Let the plant dry out without soil before potting it in fresh cactus soil in a clean pot.

See? In spite of the pricking of your thumbs, you'll find there's nothing wicked about a cactus. Here are a few other less common concerns that may be a thorn in your cactus's side:

Yellow or white patches. Diagnosis? Sunburn. No, don't break out the SPF. Just move your cactus out of the direct rays.

Pale, floppy, or weak new growth. The opposite of the yellow patches. This baby needs to soak up some sun! Increase light exposure.

Wilting even after watering. 'Fess up—did you overfertilize? Always follow fertilizer instructions. This is not a time to guesstimate.

White or gray cottony bugs. These are probably mealybugs. Get rid of them early, before they take over the whole plant. Rinse them off with water or dab them with a cotton swab dipped in rubbing alcohol.

Hard brown surface on the cactus base, like bark. This is called corking. It's a normal part of aging (the cactus equivalent of crow's-feet) and is nothing to worry about. It just means you've succeeded in keeping your cactus alive for a long time (and hey, all of us start to show some age on our skin after a while).

With any cactus, don't be too stressed if it doesn't flower right away. It can sometimes take years for a cactus to settle in and feel at home enough to flower—but when it does, those flowers tend to be spectacular: vivid colors, dramatic shapes, and long-lasting. Consider it a compliment when your cactus decides to flower.

And if you struggle with patience, you can always try forcing a bloom. Reduce their light source to no more than eight to ten hours a day for six weeks. That includes indoor light! Keep it dark at night. Just remember where in that dark you put your cactus, because it's not fun to run into unawares.

Calathea

Light: indirect light or shade
Water: water weekly or more, keeping soil moist
Soil: peaty, moist soil
Food: fertilize monthly
Pot: repot annually, good drainage

What better way to start your day than to watch your calathea open its many-splendored leaves to greet you? Or to greet the sun—if you want to be less egocentric and more accurate.

Those welcoming leaves are why indoor gardeners flock to calathea. Green and white patterns that look like they've been painted onto the smooth surface, delicate touches of pink, red edges and underbellies—there's a reason these Brazilian imports are nicknamed peacock plants, rattlesnake plants, and zebra plants. They are both decorative and alive, adding panache and a touch of nature all at once. So sign us up, especially when the plethora of different species gives us dozens of style options to choose from.

However, like many nice things, calatheas come with an asterisk: high-maintenance plant. Those delightful patterned leaves will yellow and curl with displeasure should you fail to be suitably attentive.

True to its tropical heritage, the calathea would like you to create an indoor tropical environment. The soil should be consistently damp, but not wet. A peaty mix that will retain some water is a good start, but also put yourself on a weekly (or even more frequent) watering schedule. It wants sunshine, of course, but never direct light, as this is shade vegetation, basking in dappled light filtered through taller trees. Humidity and warm temperatures will please this plant, so avoid cold rooms and AC vents, and feel free to hit it with a little mist on dry days. Maybe this is a good houseplant for your naturally more humid bathroom? With its big flat leaves, calathea is also one you'll want to keep dusted to avoid having your poor housekeeping limit its access to light.

Calathea will let you know if you're not living up to its expectations. Watch out for yellow leaves, brown tips, or curling edges when you are:

Overwatering. The calathea is picky about soil moisture levels. Yes, it should be damp. No, it should not be soggy. Like most plants, calathea will not permit sodden roots. Make sure its pot drains thoroughly and isn't collecting water in the bottom. Cut away any brown, rotten roots and repot in fresh soil.

Underwatering. Yellow leaves won't be your first sign of a parched plant. Curling edges, drooping leaves, leaves that don't close at night . . . if you've ignored these symptoms to the point where your houseplant's leaves are yellowing, please get your act together and amp up your watering schedule.

Mis-watering. Yes, the calathea will even complain about the quality of your water. The chemicals in tap water can be irritating. Let tap water sit out twenty-four hours before giving it to your plant, or use distilled water.

Withholding light. You got this calathea for its fabulous patterns, but now they're fading to yellow. Give it a little more light! Indirect light doesn't mean a dark corner.

Overlighting. That's a sunburn. Don't apply sunblock, just move it away from bright light.

Drying it out. Brown leaf tips will probably be the first sign that your calathea needs some humidity. Occasional misting, a tray of pebbles in water nearby, or a damp air location will help.

Bugging out. Spider mites, mealybugs, scale, oh my! When the big bad bugs hit your calathea, eliminate them by wiping the leaves off with an alcohol swab, rinsing them down with water, and treating them with neem oil. Sometimes just increasing the humidity can do the trick!

Being annoying. Like many teenagers, your calathea will sometimes simply find you aggravating. Yellow or curling leaves are a calathea eye roll. Did you move the pot? Rearrange companion plants? Repot? OMG, just stop, okay?

When treated with respect, calatheas grow well. Occasionally (though not commonly), they'll even flower indoors. This is a good plant for a patient, dedicated nurturer, and if you can make it through all the nitpicky details of calathea care, you deserve to be as proud as a peacock plant!

Cast Iron Plant
ASPIDISTRA ELATIOR

Light: indirect light, shade
Water: when top two inches of soil are dry
Soil: regular potting mix
Food: fertilize monthly during spring and summer
Pot: repot every three to five years, good drainage

Okay, seriously, are you really struggling to grow a plant nicknamed "cast iron" because of its reputation for indestructibility?

Just kidding. No judgment here. No one's perfect. Not even the aspidistra, which can ride its standing as "the plant that will not die" right into barroom ignominy. (It's also nicknamed "barroom plant.")

Cast iron plant gets its street cred from having survived the Victorians. As history has shown, that took some doing! Originally from the northern East Asian islands, the cast iron plant made its way to Europe more than two hundred years ago as a popular, if somewhat bourgeois, parlor plant. It graced dim barrooms and dark parlors, breathing the toxic gas lamp, coal fire, and cigar fumes, all with its sheath of dark green leaves intact and still thriving. It can grow outside. It can grow inside. It can grow in the shade. It can deal when you forget to water it for a month. It doesn't mind getting cold. It doesn't mind being hot. Insects avoid it.

But cast iron is not Teflon—some plant parent bad behaviors will stick and your aspidistra will suffer. It can handle some neglect, but not outright mistreatment.

Set your cast iron plant in a well-draining pot and position it to cheer an otherwise gloomy corner. Whatever you do, don't put it in bright sunshine. Its leaves will burn and no amount of (homegrown) aloe vera will soothe dry, brown aspidistra leaves.

It definitely needs watering—it's a plant—but it can survive a month or so without a drink. Dim lighting means lower evaporation, and this plant just likes to keep its roots on the dry side. Before you water, test the soil for any dampness about two inches below the surface. Dust off the leaves once a year (or more often if you picked a particularly dusty corner), fertilize annually, and that plant is ready to go. It grows slowly, so you probably won't have to repot very often—sometimes only once every four or five years! It's ready for a new pot only when its roots grow out of the pot. With lack of care, it can grow as high as two feet and live a long time.

There are a few problems to watch out for in even the most amiable of houseplants. Don't waste too much time feeling guilty if your cast iron plant gets huffy. Correct course and it is easily soothed.

Brown tips to the leaves. This tell is a little embarrassing. We're talking about a plant that needs watering only once a month and you forgot. Dry, brown tips usually mean that your plant is feeling a little dry. Water it and get back into the pattern of checking the soil dampness every three to four weeks.

Brown tips can also be the result of salts and minerals from hard tap water accumulating in the soil. "Rinse" the soil with a thorough watering so that water flows through the pot drainage holes. You can also try watering it with distilled water until it returns to health.

Yellow leaves. Classic. You overwatered. You neglected to neglect the neglectable houseplant. Ease up on the water! Make sure the pot is draining well so that water isn't pooling around the plant roots, rotting it from the bottom up. Don't water again until the top two inches of soil are dry to the touch.

Dry yellow or brown patches. Sunburn! The leaves are literally bleaching in direct rays. Move your aspidistra to a less intense setting. It still needs light, but indirect is best—show it some shade. Similarly, a blast of heat from a heater or fireplace will stress it out, too. Give it a stable, comfortable location.

Brown spots on the leaves. Pests usually roll right by the cast iron plant, but spots like these can be a fungus. Cut off any spotted leaves and treat the plant with an antifungal plant spray. Mealybugs and spider mites can also occasionally cause some damage in a cast iron plant. Wipe them off with alcohol swabs and treat with neem oil.

Weird purple thing near the plant's base. Not an alien invasion. This is your aspidistra's stab at a flower. Such an attempt doesn't happen often, and no one ever prized the aspidistra for its awkward flower display. Enjoy the moment, but keep loving your cast iron plant for its greenery, not its flower.

The cast iron plant has traveled far from its Asian origins and has outlived the Victorians. Honor it for its fortitude, attend to its simple needs, and you will have a beautiful and long-lived companion.

Chinese Evergreen // Philippine Evergreen
AGLAONEMA COMMUTATUM

Light: bright indirect light
Water: moist soil, regular watering
Soil: regular potting soil
Food: fertilize rarely
Pot: slightly underpot

Look, this isn't a tough one. You don't have to be pulling your hair out over a Chinese evergreen. It's a pretty chill plant (hint: it's right there in the name—*evergreen*), and as long as you can follow its super simple requests, you two are going to get along fine.

The Chinese evergreen's wide, flat leaves come in variations on a theme: green with white patterns, green with pink patterns, green with speckled patterns, green with mottled patterns. The Chinese evergreen was first imported to the United States from its Asian homeland in the 1800s. Since then, growers have experimented with different hybrids to create a multitude of leaf patterns. Pick the look that suits your style; growing needs of each varietal differ much less than their coloring.

There is one caveat on your choice of aglaonema coloring. Some houseplant experts advise that the lighter the leaf color, the more sun it will need. While this may not be a huge issue—all aglaonema plants request bright but indirect lighting—if you have a more dimly lit space with little of that cheerful sunlight during the day, you might consider a more richly hued varietal.

A few other directions from this evergreen:

Brown or yellow leaves. This is usually your plant cueing you in that something is up with your watering technique. Brown suggests too little water. Your plant is literally drying out on the edges because there's no moisture for it to consume. Poke a finger in the soil. Is it dry and dusty? Water! However, yellow leaves start to show up when you're watering too much. Water is pooling around the roots, rotting your plant from the bottom up, and yellowing the leaves as it drowns. Again, test the soil. Is it soggy? Let it dry! Make sure water is able to drain well from holes in the pot base.

Limp. When your plant droops and looks depressed, that may be a cry for water similar to when its leaves brown. Get yourself on a regular watering schedule (most houseplants favor weekly waterings) and get used to testing the soil moisture. Chinese evergreen likes consistently moist (not wet or dry) soil.

If you have accidentally skipped a watering and your plant friend is looking rather wilted or brown, be aware that watering it now, while necessary for survival, can also cause it stress. A stressed-out plant will drop leaves. Don't worry! They'll grow back. Just take it as a passive-aggressive criticism of your watering technique.

Patchy. A Chinese evergreen *will not* tolerate cold. If you live in a location where the temperature drops during certain seasons, make sure your home ambience stays more consistent. We're not sure why you'd want to sit around in a house that's less than 60 degrees, but your aglaonema definitely will not want to. If you see dark, greasy-looking patches on the leaves, that's what a chilled Chinese evergreen looks like. Move it away from a cold window or adjust the thermostat a few degrees.

Leaf curling. Aglaonema leaves are flat and smooth, so if the edges start to curl in, your plant is not pleased with you. Low humidity and chilly temperatures can make its leaves curl. Mist it, warm it up, but also check for pests. Mealybugs are the most likely pest, sucking nutrients that would feed the curled leaves out of stems.

Leggy. An aglaonema prefers a bushy look. If it's looking stretched out and long-stemmed, it might be time to change the pot. While it likes a pot that hugs the roots (popularly known as underpotting), at some point it just runs out of space to grow. Move it to an only slightly larger pot and prune back scraggly stems to encourage it to regrow with a fuller figure.

As your aglaonema succeeds, so may you. This is a good luck plant, reputed to bring favorable fortune to its grower. Pay close attention to its few needs and you two will have a happy future together.

Coin Plant

Pilea peperomioides

Light: bright indirect—occasionally direct—sunlight
Water: water when dry, one to two weeks
Soil: regular potting mix
Food: fertilize monthly during spring and summer
Pot: repot annually, ensuring good drainage

Who would say no to a little coin? More than a little, if you invest in a coin plant. A charming indoor foliage plant with its circular (coin-shaped) leaves, it is also a fantastic self-propagator. Get yourself a *Pilea peperomioides* and watch your money plant grow.

The coin plant has almost as many names as it does offspring: Chinese money plant, pancake plant, UFO plant, and even missionary plant, presumably a reference to its reputed travel history. Supposedly a Norwegian missionary brought it home from China in the 1940s and shared its progeny with friends.

China and Norway are wildly different environments, so it won't surprise you to learn that the coin plant adapts well to new surroundings and is not a challenging houseplant to maintain. Direct sun will scorch it and gloomy shade will sometimes result in smaller leaves, so perch it somewhere with good light (but nothing too intense). It definitely prefers to dry out a bit between waterings, so select a pot and soil with good drainage. Those pancake leaves go limp when it needs more water. The leaves also need regular dusting, so misting your coin plant or giving it a hearty shower will help.

Now for the fun part: repotting. This doesn't need to be done more than once a year, giving your plant plenty of time to produce pups, those mini coin plants that emerge from the soil all around the parent plant. When you (gently) extract the coin plant from its pot, disentangle the baby plants from the roots and get the new guys started in their very own small pots with some damp soil. (The parent plant can move to a slightly larger pot.) Now you have a ton of coin. Share with friends or hoard it.

It may be relatively easy to care for, but nobody likes it when their money plant depreciates. Watch your coin plant stash for:

Limp, droopy leaves. Is the potting mix dry, too? Just add water. Those leaves will perk back up to pancake shape after a good drink.

Yellow leaves, black stems. Ugh, you overwatered. Coin plants like to dry out a little. If your pot is not draining well or you're just pumping in too much of the wet stuff, the roots will get waterlogged and start to rot. Stop watering immediately. Your plant may revive and turn green again if you give it a chance to grow fresh roots. Remove any yellow or black dead growth to prevent fungus and bacteria spread.

Dry brown leaf patches. Ouch! This one is too hot. Move it out of the direct sun to an area with good light, but not harsh rays. The burned leaves won't recover, but the plant will, and those leaves can be removed.

Small leaves, long stems. We did say *good* light, not low light. When it doesn't get enough light, the coin plant produces smaller leaves and leggy stems. It will also grow fewer pups. A little closer to the window, please! You might also consider periodically rotating your plant; it bends toward the sun, so shift it to keep growth symmetrical.

Like most indoor plants, *Pilea peperomioides* needs to watch out for pests—the usual suspects that make their way through your indoor jungle: mealybugs, spider mites, scale, fungus. Keep an eye out for unwelcome visitors, but the coin plant is not especially at risk from infestation. Remove any bugs with alcohol swabs or a neem oil spray.

Coin plant is a good luck plant, and since it rapidly produces additional plants for your collection, your green thumb can grow without a sizable investment of coin. That's money in the bank. Or in the terra-cotta pot.

Coleus

Plectranthus scutellarioides or *Coleus scutellarioides*

Light: bright indirect light

Water: consistently moist soil

Soil: well-draining potting mix

Food: not necessary, but can take slow-release fertilizer pellets in spring

Pot: repot to encourage a larger plant, or prune leaves and refresh soil

The painted nettle, the poor man's croton, an ever-changing Latin title—let's just call it the coleus and fall in love with its fascinating foliage and simple to-do list.

Coleus has been a popular outdoor border garden favorite since Victorian times, known for its bushy and delightfully varied leaves of green, maroon, chartreuse, pink, and red arranged in a multitude of patterns; there are hundreds of hybridized versions of this Asian native plant. And it is more than happy to share that splendor inside as your new favorite houseplant.

Proper coleus care demands bright light, though it should avoid direct afternoon rays. It wants moist soil all the time, so water consistently and don't let it dry out completely in between. Humidity, the other half of keeping moisture levels reliable, is important, so keep it in a damper spot like a bathroom or add a little spritz of water to its regular care. This is not a large-scale indoor plant—in fact, it will look better if you prune it—so it won't need to be repotted unless it becomes rootbound.

Pruning is the key to keeping a coleus looking good longer than a season. As it grows up, it starts to get leggy. Pinching off new growth will push it to grow a bushier shape. Pinching off flower stalks is especially important if you want the plant to keep putting its growing energy into its fabulous foliage.

To keep it growing bushy and beautiful, avoid:

Wilted leaves, fading to a dry yellow. Check the top inch or two of soil. Dry? Time to water. Coleus likes its soil moist all the time.

Droopy yellow leaves, brown leaves. Isn't it confusing how quickly a moisture-loving plant can suffer from overwatering? Yellow leaves are the first sign of too much soggy soil. Check the soil. Does it feel muddy to the touch? Your plant needs to dry out more between waterings. Poor drainage is the most common cause of overwatering. Your plant's pot must have good drainage holes and a potting soil that drains well. If the soil gets dense and packed down over time, replace it with fresh stuff. If your plant is overwatered too often, its roots will start to rot, and it will be hard to save.

Faded leaf colors. This is a lighting issue. You love your coleus for its bright leaves, right? It's distressing when they start to disappear. Give a coleus bright but indirect light—this is not a shade plant. It can take more direct morning light, but those afternoon direct rays will fade leaves as fast as shade will.

Yellowing leaves, roots pushing through soil. Congratulations—you have maintained your coleus long enough for it to outgrow its pot. When the roots push out of the soil, it's rootbound. Move it to a newer, bigger pot (with good drainage) and reward it with fresh potting mix.

Curling, misshapen leaves. Take a look at the undersides of the leaves. If you see a gray or purple growth on the leaf, you've probably got downy mildew, caused by too much humidity and water on the leaves. To treat it, remove any leaves where you see the growth and keep a close eye on other leaves to prevent spread.

Mealybugs, aphids, and spider mites. You can spot these little guys infecting your coleus if you are taking the time to look over its foliage regularly (maybe while you're pruning). Wipe them away with rubbing alcohol or treat with neem oil. The earlier you catch them, the faster you can get rid of them.

Even the best coleus and even the best plant parent can sometimes fail. If you realize your coleus may not survive, why not carry on its traditions with a little quick and easy propagation? You can grow a mini-me coleus from your existing plant with the exact leaf patterns and colors, something you won't get from seeds. Simply cut off a four- to six-inch stem above a leaf node and set it in water, taking care to keep any leaves out of the water, and wait for roots to sprout. There you are: brand-new coleus!

Corn Plant

Dracaena fragrans

Light:	bright indirect light
Water:	consistently moist soil
Soil:	potting mix with good drainage
Food:	diluted fertilizer monthly in spring and summer
Pot:	repot every one to two years, using fresh soil

A tropical African plant, this favorite of the popular houseplant genus *Dracaena* gives you all the island vacation vibes of a palm combined with the ease of a plant well-suited to an indoor lifestyle.

Corn plants grow as high as four to six feet in indoor containers, rising from one or more central canes (you'd call them trunks if you didn't know better) into long narrow leaves reminiscent of those on a stalk of corn. They like a soothingly steady environment—even temperatures, consistent light access, and a regular watering schedule.

Water will be the fussiest point for a corn plant. They like a steadily moist soil (no drying out in between showers) and have a preference for distilled water or rainwater, especially if your tap water is high in chlorine and fluoride. They prefer a richer soil, so use a rich potting soil to start and then fertilize during the summer growing season. If your dracaena is suffering from lack of humidity—perhaps in a really dry winter—set its pot in a tray of wet pebbles and lightly mist its long leaves.

As your corn plant ages over the years, the lowest variegated green leaves will naturally turn yellow and can be removed without causing you too much concern. That's just their life span. There are bigger problems to anticipate:

Brown leaf tips, yellowing leaves. Overwatering is the biggest danger to your corn plant. Wait until the surface and even the top inch of soil feels dry before you water again (but no more than the top inch!). Use a pot that is not overly big for the plant and check for good drainage holes.

Confusingly, underwatered plants also have brown leaf tips, so this is where you pay attention to what *you* have been doing, not relying on the plant to spell it out for you. Is the soil bone dry and crumbly? Underwatered. Is the soil soggy and clammy wet? Overwatered. If you leave a corn plant wet for too long, it will eventually start to lose its leaves. If it progresses to the point where the roots are wet and smelly and the cane is mushy, it has root rot and will probably survive best from propagating a cutting.

Those brown leaf tips can also be caused by fluoride in your tap water. Or low humidity. Investigate through the process of elimination and cut off the ugly brown edges without damaging the plant.

Faded leaf variegation. Corn plant leaves are green with paler strips of yellow or light green. When these patterns start to fade away, your plant is trying to tell you it needs more light. Persistently low light conditions will stunt its growth.

Wilting, inward-curling leaves, brown patches. Direct sun doesn't suit a tropical plant like this one, however. Its leaves will wilt and curl inward to escape the burning rays. Stick to indirect light only.

Damaged leaves. Spider mites, thrips, and scale all like to make a corn plant their home. The best prevention is to go on the offensive: regularly dust your corn plant, gently wiping down the leaves, and pests will have nowhere to squat. Insecticides will take care of those that slip through your defenses.

Because of their tall, columnar grace, corn plants make popular office and houseplants. They look imposing, but don't take up much space. If over the years your corn plant gets a little too tall, simply cut off the top of the cane. New leaves will sprout out just below the cut.

A smaller alternative is a close cousin of *Dracaena fragrans*, *Dracaena deremensis*. Similar corn-leaf style, but in a stubbier, bushier shape. Care plans are similar, with a special eye toward water quality—pick distilled water for this one, too.

CROTON

CODIAEUM VARIEGATUM

Light: bright indirect light (very bright!)
Water: water weekly, keeping soil moist
Soil: regular potting mix
Food: fertilize sparingly, every other month
Pot: repot when rootbound, good drainage

What's the first rule of croton? Don't mess with a croton. However, since you have decided to do so, the second rule is: Be prepared to face the consequences.

We can't blame you for delighting in the croton for your indoor jungle. Their thick, shiny leaves lend a polished, finished appearance to your space and come in a dazzling array of colors: green (of course), but also orange, red, and yellow. It's the brilliance of fall foliage all year long, right in your own home. There are hundreds of varieties of this Southeast Asian tropical plant, and you have probably seen them as popular fillers of indoor planters in malls and public buildings.

But popularity does not equal easy companionship. The croton is demanding and particular. It needs consistent watering (no vacations or carelessness permitted!), humidity, bright light, and good dusting. Another concern to add to the croton list: The sap can be toxic, causing skin irritation and eczema, not to mention being disastrous for a nibbling pet. Get the environment and commitment right, however, and the croton can grow to about three feet high indoors, full and leafy.

The best thing you can do for your croton is to listen carefully, identify its specific needs, and stick to that list of needs with the kind of devotion and faithfulness a beauty like this expects.

Fading colors. You love your croton for its fabulous red and orange colors, right? How distressing, then, when those colors start to fade in brilliance. Your croton is trying to tell you that it needs to soak up some sun. Heavy shade won't work. Move it closer to a well-lit window—not directly into hot rays, but with a reliable supply of six to eight hours of bright light a day. Wipe down those smooth leaves when dust builds up so sunlight isn't blocked by grubbiness! If you find gray patches on the leaves, however, that's not a dust bunny—you have let too much direct sun burn the leaves.

Falling leaves. Its colors may remind you of autumn leaf-peeping, but croton leaves are not supposed to fall off. Your croton is complaining about moisture levels. Water often enough to keep the soil consistently moist. Misting is a good idea if you have an especially dry climate.

You might also see **dry brown leaves** when your croton is thirsty for more water and sultry air.

Spider mites. The drier the air, the more likely your croton is to acquire a case of spider mites. How do you keep your plant safe? Try misting your plant, placing trays of wet pebbles to gradually evaporate near it, and (in extremely dry settings) running a humidifier in the room with it. Wiping the plant's leaves down with alcohol swabs and treating them with neem oil should help stop an infestation already in progress.

vibrant colors =
healthy

faded colors =
needs indirect sunlight

falling leaves =
not enough water

twisted leaves =
excess fertilizer

Yellow leaves and dropping leaves. This is a croton temper tantrum. Did you recently repot? Have you moved its location? Did you look at it funny the other day? The croton can respond with sallow coloring, and by flinging off leaves. Be patient. Treat it with kindness and consistency, and within a few weeks it should get itself together and start growing well again.

Wilting. We know what you're thinking—a wilting plant needs more water. The croton, however, develops that limp, sad look when it gets *too much* water. Overwatering and/or poor drainage are keeping the soil soggy and the croton's roots are rotting. It might be best to repot into a clean, dry pot (with drainage holes!) and be a little less generous with the watering can. Your goal is damp, not marshy, soil.

Twisting leaves. Yes, there are some cultivars, like the 'Mammy', that feature twisted leaves. However, if you're caring for a variety known for smooth, flat leaves, like the 'Petra', get nervous when those leaves twist or bend. You may be overfertilizing. Check the soil around the plant's base—do you see white deposits? That could be excess salts and fertilizer. Water your croton thoroughly, and if it is still struggling, consider refreshing the soil. Then hold off on the fertilizer. Crotons are happy with the soil they have and at most want fertilizing every other month, or even just quarterly.

Have some fun with this one—croton's leaf shapes are as uniquely varied as their hues: oval, narrow, or twisted. Select from great varietal names like 'Dreadlocks', 'Mona Lisa', 'Petra', and so many more.

CROWN OF THORNS

EUPHORBIA MILII

Light: three to four hours of bright direct sun

Water: water thoroughly when top inch of soil is dry

Soil: fast-draining cactus or succulent soil

Food: fertilize every two weeks to a month, diluted solution

Pot: repot every two years, good drainage

Despite a vivid and dramatic name and a vivid and dramatic appearance, the crown of thorns, or Christ plant, is an easygoing plant with simple needs.

Getting past that name and appearance to attend to those needs is the challenge. Let's start with the name: it's a description, not a recommendation. Do not wear this as a crown. Its sharp, black-barbed stems are rumored to have formed the crown inflicted on Christ before his crucifixion; the plant's red bracts, then, represent drops of Jesus's blood. This is an unlikely origin story. Most biblical scholars point the finger at the jujube tree as the source of Christ's torture instead of a crown of thorns bush. As *Euphorbia milii* hails from Madagascar and was introduced to Western gardeners in the nineteenth century by one Baron Milius (hence its Latin name), we have to agree with those scholars.

But the plant's look does live up to its name. Admire the clusters of brilliant red, orange, or yellow bracts encasing the flowers, but keep your fingers away from those intense thorny stems. In fact, just wear gloves when approaching a crown of thorns—its sap is a skin irritant and it's poisonous to pets.

If you're not scared away by this fierce little succulent, remember what we said up front: This is a low-maintenance houseplant! How so?

- **It likes direct sun.** Struggling to find that nebulous "indirect" light is not an issue with this houseplant. Pop it in a windowsill and let it soak up the sun for at least three hours a day.
- **It's not picky about water.** Forgot a shower? No worries. Crown of thorns can handle a dry spell. Water it thoroughly (so water flows out of the pot's drainage holes) and then leave it alone again until its top inch of soil is dry.
- **Humidity? What's that?** Crown of thorns won't require that ubiquitous tray of damp pebbles or misting. If you're comfortable with the ambient indoor climate, it is, too.

Even the easiest plant has its bad days, however:

Root rot. This is THE big issue for a crown of thorns. Lots of plant care missteps can cause it: too frequent watering, ineffective watering, poor-quality soil, a pot that doesn't drain well, or a pot that is too big. So if your Christ plant has yellow leaves, starts to lose its leaves, or even gets limp, mushy stems, go through this root-rot checklist.

1. Wait to water until the top inch of soil is quite dry—in the winter months, when it gets less sun exposure, you can wait for the top *two* inches to dry out.
2. Don't just dribble in a little water. Let it flow! Water until water pours out of the drainage holes and then tip any excess out of the saucer.
3. If it's been a while since you repotted, get this baby some fresh soil; soil that's been in the pot for a few years can stop draining well.
4. Drainage holes. Seriously, these are something your pot *must* include.
5. In a pot that is too big for the plant, the soil takes longer to dry out all through and can leave too much moisture around the roots. Fit the pot to the plant—it should be a couple of inches bigger than the root ball.

Of course, crown of thorns can be underwatered as well. If you've been stingy with the water lately and your plant is not blooming regularly, get back on a weekly watering schedule to encourage growth.

Too much sun. Curled leaves and brown edges on the leaves can mean it's getting hot in here. Morning sun works well for a crown of thorns, but as the day passes and the sun heat intensifies, your plant can be getting well more than the three to four hours of direct sun it needs. Move it to somewhere a little less intense.

Household pests are not a frequent problem for crown of thorns. Perhaps they got the memo about its being thorny and poisonous? But keep an eye out for spider mites and mealybugs, especially if your crown of thorns hangs out with other houseplants a lot.

Well tended and respected, the indoor crown of thorns can grow several feet high and live for many years. Just brush aside that overwrought name—and keep your hands from brushing its thorny stems!

Dragon Tree

Dracaena marginata

Light: part shade to full sun

Water: water when top half of soil is dry, up to three weeks

Soil: well-drained, loose, peaty soil

Food: fertilize rarely, diluted solution in the spring

Pot: repot when rootbound, two to three years

Fear not the dragon. That awesome terrifying mythical creature breathing fire in your mind translates in plant form to a reliable, steadfast, and mellow indoor dragon tree. Popular for generations as an easy and handsome houseplant, this species of the far-reaching *Dracaena* genus is about as far as you can get from Smaug.

Is the dragon tree scary? No! It handles a variety of lighting, is undemanding with its watering schedule, and isn't fussy about temperature or humidity.

Is the dragon tree a fire-breather? No! In fact, the dragon tree purifies the air around it, improving your air quality in modest silence.

Is the dragon tree a legend? No! It's been considered cool since the sixties and has hung around long after bell-bottoms exited the scene.

However, there are rumors that the *Dracaena marginata* and its cousin *Dracaena draco* appeared on the island of Madagascar grown from the blood of a defeated mighty dragon. We can't prove that's not true . . .

Regardless, you'll find dragon tree communication relatively stress-free, with or without the One Ring. Its spiky leaves grow like vivid green and purplish-red ribbons atop a long central stem to lend a look of unique spareness to sophisticated room decor. As it ages (and as you prune it), it can add extra stems branching off from the original stem to resemble a small tree. This plant will last you many years, as it is gracefully tolerant of neglect and inconsistent living environments. How much light does it need? It's not too picky. Full sun can work, as can shade. How much water does it need? Not a lot. It's happiest when it can dry out well between waterings. How much humidity does it need? It doesn't really care. Apart from freezing or super hot temperatures and climates, it's adaptable to human comfort levels.

You can totally tame this dragon, right? However, you want to do your best for your little dragon, so here are the few things it has to say when it's not feeling at its best:

Brown tips to the leaves. Listed as drought tolerant, *Dracaena marginata* should be more specific: drought preferred. If you are watering weekly in a pot without good drainage or soil, water will settle in a bog around your plant's poor roots. It needs to dry out! Only water when the top few inches of soil (up to even the top half) are dry. Still seeing brown tips? Your dragon tree may be objecting to the level of salt and fluoride in your water supply. Let the water sit out overnight before watering so that the chemicals in it can evaporate, or try using distilled water. Chemicals can also build up if you've been overfertilizing. Never fertilize in the winter; always use a slow-release or diluted solution, and give your plant's soil a good rinse (let water flow through the soil) if you fear you have been heavy-handed with the food.

Yellow leaves or brown spots. You've gone a little too far on the drought. Your plant is thirsty. Please water thoroughly, until water is flowing out of the pot's drainage holes. However, if you see just a few leaves near the base of the leafy crown starting to yellow, bend, and dry, they may just be reaching the end of their life cycle. Remove dead leaves and enjoy the new green ones sprouting from the center of the crown. As the dragon tree grows, its stem will get longer and longer as the crown keeps producing new leaves and shedding old ones.

Small, limp leaves, with less color. Too much shade. While the dragon tree can handle some shade, it does need consistent access to bright light to be able to grow properly. Move it to a sunnier location.

Dry brown patches. Too much sun! Some direct sun can work for the dragon tree, but too much and it will get singed. Moderate the amount of light it's getting each day (this may change depending on the time of year).

Slowing growth, roots pushing against the pot and drainage holes. This plant needs a new pot! You should also check to see if its soil is loose or compact. Compact soil won't drain well when you water and indicates that it's time for a change. Move to a slightly larger pot and get some fresh loose, peaty soil.

Well loved, the dragon tree grows happily up to six feet indoors. If that's a little large for your space, you can prune it back. Cut off its stem at a 45-degree angle at the height you'd like it. It looks awful for a while—just a barren stem—but soon it will pop out smaller branches just below where you cut it and those will keep on growing into new crowns of leaves.

Or you can just learn to live with a large dragon.

Dumbcane

Dieffenbachia

Light: part shade to bright indirect light
Water: water consistently when top inch of soil is dry
Soil: well-drained, peaty soil
Food: fertilize monthly, diluted solution
Pot: repot annually, good drainage

Let's get this straight up front: Don't chew your dieffenbachia. We're not sure why anyone ever wanted to, but it appears to be a popular enough activity to have warranted its common name, dumbcane. No, not dumb for the stupidity of eating a houseplant, dumb as in unable to speak, because the needle-shaped crystals (called raphides) contained in the leaves will cause your tongue and mouth to swell, rendering you unable to speak. This is temporary, if silly, for you, but it's deadly for your pet, so keep dumb animals and dumbcane absolutely separate.

Now that you've decided not to chew on your dieffenbachia, you can focus your attention on its care. Its big, flat green leaves with white veins and patterns emerging from a sturdy central stem make it an attractive part of your indoor decor. As a bonus, its relatively simple needs make it an appealing choice. Dumbcane is a tropical plant of South and Central American origins. It prefers humid settings, moist but well-drained soils, and indirect light.

Its need for humidity makes dieffenbachia a good candidate for a humid setting, like a bathroom (also a good location to suit its request for indirect light). If you don't really want a dumbcane next to the toilet, introduce some sultry air wherever you settle your houseplant. Misting provides good temporary damp air, but for consistent humidity, favor it with the constant evaporation from a tray of wet pebbles.

Dieffenbachia is a little coquettish in its communications, favoring yellow leaves as an answer to all concerns. Let's sort through a few common problems.

Yellow leaves. The overwatering versus underwatering debate rages on, as both conditions make a dieffenbachia break out in yellow. The top inch of soil should be dry before you water, no more, no less. If overwatering (or a soggy pot with poor drainage and too much space) is your problem, sometimes the dumbcane will get extremely upset and start weeping. Literally— droplets fall from its leaves. It is desperately trying to excrete excess water in its sap. Let it dry out.

Yellowing can also mean it's hungry. Fertilizing monthly is a good start, but it will also need its soil perked up every now and then. Repot with fresh, rich, peaty soil once a year.

Yellow or brown drooping leaves. This dumbcane is *too* hot. Excess sun exposure will stress it out. It's accustomed to the dappled shade filtering between the tall trees of its tropical homeland. Find it a shadier corner.

However, **drooping leaves or dropping its lower leaves** can also mean it's too cold. You don't enjoy a home below 65 degrees, do you? Neither does your Southern Hemisphere plant friend. Warm the place up a bit and keep dumbcane out of drafty, chilly areas (like in the direct blast of an air conditioner).

Roots pushing out of the drainage holes. Rootbound! Time to move to a bigger pot. This is also a great time to refresh the soil and make sure it has the right amount of growing space in the pot. When you remove the plant from its old pot, gently tap out old soil from around its roots before placing it in its new home. The new pot shouldn't offer more than two extra inches of space for fresh soil around the root ball. When a pot is too big, the soil can't dry out well around the plant roots, causing root rot. And by now you know your pot needs drainage holes, right? No soggy bottoms.

Spider mites or aphids. With its wide, flat leaves, the dumbcane is easy to check for pests. Look underneath the leaf and at the stem for intruders, and gently wipe any away with neem oil. If you keep up with occasional dusting, you can spot pests before they become a problem.

These are all treatable problems, especially if you pay attention to watering. With a reliable companion like this, why would you want to chew its leaves? Get yourself a mint and enjoy the dumbcane for its beauty, not its flavor.

Echeveria

Light: bright indirect light
Water: water when soil is dry, drain well
Soil: cactus or succulent soil
Food: fertilize at most annually, very diluted solution
Pot: only when outgrowing pot, good drainage

The cutie-pies of the houseplant world! Echeverias are neat, perfectly arranged, adorable succulents. You don't need to be a houseplant genius to care for them, and with a dazzling array of colors in their repertoire, they always add a special something to the home. To begin with, they look so perfect! Unlike many houseplants, shedding leaves (ahem, ferns) or trailing vines (pothos, philodendrons) all over the place, echeverias will remain composed and compact in a tidy rosette of plump leaves.

Then there is the plethora of options in size, shape, and color; there is a perfect echeveria out there for everyone. Pick a favorite color: pale green 'Mexican Snowball', blush-pink 'Dusty Rose', silvery 'Ghost' echeveria, or dark purple 'Black Prince'. Or pick a favorite shape: paddle-shaped 'Perle von Nurnberg', scooped and folded 'Topsy Turvy', fuzzy 'Chenille Plant', or crinkly 'Crinoline Ruffles'.

Lastly, echeverias make plant care so low stress. Have you watered enough? Have you watered too much? Is there enough light? These are questions the echeveria answers clearly, without undue fuss and without a lot of extra attention.

Echeverias do well with a bit of neglect. Most of the time, when you pass an echeveria, it prefers that you just keep moving and not get involved. When it does need care, the rules are simple: Water when the soil is *completely* dry, give it bright but indirect light, and keep it in a pot with porous soil and excellent drainage. That's it! You've got this.

When you go wrong, the echeveria doesn't force you to guess what it's thinking.

Wrinkled, wilted, dry leaves. No, don't put your night cream on the leaves. This plant just needs water! Pour it on until water flows out of the drainage holes. Make sure all the water has dripped out before replacing the pot in a saucer or decorative pot. Otherwise, you will get . . .

Yellow, colorless, soggy leaves. Way, way too much water. If you have a watering compulsion, a succulent will suffer. It needs the soil to dry out completely between waterings. And if that pot doesn't drain properly, or the soil retains too much moisture packed in around the roots, the roots will rot, causing yellow leaves. An overly large pot, too, tends to hold on to moisture longer, the extra soil taking longer to dry out than is good for an echeveria's well-being.

Rot. When you have really abused the watering schedule, those rotten roots will spread into a rotten plant. Black spots, soft or slimy sections, and a bad smell mean the whole echeveria is rotten to the core. This may be past saving. If you can cut away the rotten spots, do so ASAP. If you can't, cut away any healthy leaves or sections of the plant to propagate a new one. Hopefully you'll do better on the next round.

Stretched out, leggy, bending toward light. This means not enough light. The echeveria needs around six hours of indirect bright light a day, so move it closer to the sunshine.

Crunchy brown patches. Now you've moved it too close to the sunlight. Yes, give it lots of light, but always keep it indirect or your plant will end up with brown patches. Echeverias don't tan, they burn.

Bent or misshapen leaves. You may be playing host to someone other than an echeveria, one of the usual suspects: mealybugs, scale, or aphids. When bugs bite your plant, they can suck the moisture from that juicy succulent, causing limp or bent leaves. Wipe leaves off with soapy water (then rinse the plant down) or a mild insecticide and consider repotting with a clean pot and fresh soil.

One more thing to love about echeverias? How cute they are when they're propagating (you can't say that about most species)! Since you quickly mastered any risks to echeveria health, you are ready to start a new family of these sweet succulents. This is also a good solution if your best efforts to solve problems have failed, because you need only one leaf of a dying echeveria to start anew. Pop a leaf off the stem (be gentle!). Place the leaf on the surface of a new pot of soil in bright (but indirect) light and wait a few weeks. Roots will start to grow after two or three weeks, and then a tiny rosette of new leaves will grow at the original leaf's base. Don't break off the old leaf—the new plant will use it for nutrients as it grows until the old leaf shrivels up. Water only when the soil is dry, as you would a grown-up succulent, and spend some time getting to know your new baby echeveria.

Elephant Ear

Alocasia

Light: bright indirect light
Water: consistently moist soil
Soil: well-draining potting mix
Food: liquid fertilizer during spring and summer
Pot: repot annually

Yes, it does resemble an elephant's ear. No, this does not mean you'll have hairy gray pachyderms dominating your home decor.

Alocasia's leaves are ruffled and wrinkled in the heart shape usually attached to Dumbo, but these dark green, veined, shiny leaves attach to long stems, growing in clusters that make them a showstopper of an indoor plant.

Elephant ear grows from a rhizome (or tuber) that likes to stay moist. Water when the top inch or so of soil is dry, keeping that soil damp at all times, but without allowing water to collect in a muddy puddle from poor drainage. This plant likes partial shade. It wants bright sun to reach those big, colorful leaves, but not direct sun. Repot your elephant ear once a year. It feeds heavily, and even if you fertilize regularly, it will be happy with some fresh soil every year—and it will grow larger as it graduates to a bigger pot! Each new leaf is bigger than the last.

Watch those ears for:

Drooping leaves. They start by looking limp, then get brown edges, slowly turning yellow and brown and shriveling away. This is a thirsty plant. Water

72

right away, giving it a good soak to rehydrate the soil. Elephant ear doesn't like drought and will struggle with stress if it's allowed to dry out.

Increasing humidity can also help keep those leaves perky. Use a tray of damp pebbles to add a little evaporated moisture to the air.

Yellow leaves. If the soil is soggy and your elephant's ears are turning yellow or brown, your plant is probably suffering from root rot caused by overwatering. You need a pot with good drainage and a soil that will let water flow on through. The soil should stay damp, not wet.

Another possibility is poor lighting. While preferring some shade, elephant ears still need a bright light close by! And don't forget to dust those big old ears so plenty of light can reach the chlorophyll.

Brown patches. Direct light, however, will give those leaves a sunburn.

Brown or black spots with a yellow rim. Fungal infections usually show up if your plant is overwatered—too much moisture is the perfect environment for a fungus to grow. Give your plant good air circulation and don't water until the top inch of soil is dry.

Yellow spots or leaves. Bug bites. When spider mites, scale, or mealybugs go after an *Alocasia* already stressed by poor watering or lighting, they can quickly attack by sucking out its green juices. Keep an eye out for pests and remove them with an insecticide as soon as possible!

Yellowing older leaves. If the oldest leaves on your plant are turning yellow, don't stress about it. This is part of its natural process and nothing to worry about. Let your plant expend its energy on growing new leaves and remove the old yellow ones.

There are dozens of varieties of *Alocasia* in different color patterns. Some are a contrast of dark green with pale green ribs, while others turn reddish. However, keep an eye on your Latin. There are also other plants nicknamed elephant ear, but these are entirely different plants with wide leaves, coming from other genera: *Caladium, Colocasia,* and *Xanthosoma.* These are all pretty, with wide green leaves, but with somewhat different styles and growing needs. When acquiring the elephant's ear profiled here, be sure to ask for it by its proper name: *Alocasia.*

Fiddle-Leaf Fig

Ficus lyrata

Light: bright indirect light

Water: water consistently, keeping soil moist

Soil: regular potting soil, well-draining

Food: fertilize quarterly, only in spring or summer

Pot: repot or refresh soil annually

It's not easy being the must-have houseplant of the decade. Magazine spreads, TV features, social media highlights—the fiddle-leaf fig never asked for this kind of fame. It enjoyed modest success in its tropical African homeland and even an occasional appearance in a humid Florida landscape scene, but this kind of ubiquity has left it feeling a little . . . stressed.

You really can't go anywhere these days without spotting the fiddle-leaf fig. Everyone's got to try it. But ask those enthusiasts how their fig is a year later and there's a good chance they will have already killed it. This is not a plant for the casual indoor gardener. It needs care, respect, and the kind of dedicated attention most pop stars require from their staff.

It's easy to see why the fiddle-leaf is so beloved in spite of its overbearing popularity and diva-like demands. Those huge glossy leaves shaped like lyres or fiddles, which earn it its Latin and common names, growing atop a slender trunk in a full, lovely crown—*anyone* would covet a houseplant that good-lookin'.

Are you that anyone? Great! Just know what you're getting into and your fiddle-leaf can flourish.

Let's start by re-creating its tropical origins. It needs steady moisture levels, sometimes requiring watering two or three times a week in drier areas or seasons. The goal is to keep its soil always damp, though never soggy. It's used to diffused light, filtering through taller trees, but not actual shade. An east-facing window would be ideal, offering lots of bright light, but not a direct blast. Warm, humid air is a must. Wild swings in temperature, such as proximity to a heater or AC vent might provide, are not a good idea. You can provide extra humidity with a tray of wet pebbles and by regularly misting the air around your fiddle-leaf. It will need repotting once a year, since a happy *Ficus lyrata* is a fast-growing *Ficus lyrata*, but it may not respond well to the stress of moving. Be patient after a big change like that and expect some leaf loss. When your plant has gotten too big to reasonably repot (you're not bringing a crane into your living room, are you?), you can still dig out old soil from around its roots and refresh it with new soil once a year.

Those are all the things you can do right. Not so bad, is it? Then how do so many fiddle-leaf fig owners go wrong? Lack of stick-to-itiveness. Here's what you need to watch for:

Brown edges. Dry brown crinkly edges to sad, droopy leaves aren't a sign of depression in a fiddle-leaf—they're a sign of thirst. Get that plant some water and keep it moist.

Yellow leaves. The fiddle-leaf fig will start to yellow when it's not getting enough light. Find a brighter source! And remember to gently wipe down those huge leaves when they get dusty so the sunshine can make its way through to the plant's chlorophyll.

Dropping leaves. Like many in the *Ficus* genus, the fiddle-leaf fig will abruptly shed its gorgeous leaves when it is unhappy. There are several likely culprits for this kind of stress:

1. Be honest. Are you a good houseplant waterer? Check your fig's soil. If the top three inches are dry, add some water. If the soil is a muddy mess, for goodness' sake, stop overwatering.

2. We warned you about maintaining the right temperature. If you let your fiddle-leaf get chilled or overheated or parched from dry air, reread care directions and get your home environment back on track.

3. Location matters to a fig. That is, staying in the same location. If you move your fiddle-leaf, whether during repotting or just to a more decorative corner of your home, expect it to react by dropping leaves. They'll grow back!

Brown spots. These are the worst. You picked out this gorgeous plant for its big green leaves, and now those leaves are spoiled with brown spots or patches. Check for:

1. **Overwatering.** Soil that is wet and boggy from too frequent watering or a pot that's not draining properly will cause your fiddle-leaf's roots to rot. If you see yellowing leaves or brown spots, this should be the first thing you check. Make sure the pot is draining

thoroughly after a watering, and then let it dry a bit more between waterings.

2. **Infection.** Bacterial or fungal infections also cause brown spots. It can be hard to spot the difference between infections and root rot, so err on the side of caution—carefully remove damaged leaves. If you continue to see problems, consider repotting with fresh soil and a clean pot.

3. **Infestation.** Tiny little brown spots may be the work of tiny little pests. Aphids, spider mites, scale, mealybugs—when these problem guests bite and suck the juices of your poor plant, it will leave brown spots. Use a diluted neem oil to wipe off intruders and remove particularly infested leaves to prevent any spread.

4. **Sunburn.** These spots will actually look paler and patchier and are caused by direct sun burning your poor fig's leaves. Move it out of the direct rays.

5. **Fertilizer burn.** *Ficus lyrata* is not a big feeder. Fertilizing too often—especially during the winter—leaves it with too much chemical buildup. Fertilize more rarely, and if you are concerned you may have overdone it, water thoroughly, flushing water through the soil until it pours out of drainage holes, rinsing away impurities.

Feeling daunted? None of this is beyond your reach, just potentially beyond your commitment level. If your fiddle-leaf fig is telling you, "It's not me, it's you," swallow your ego and take the hint. Beauty and popularity take some work.

Goldfish Plant
Nematanthus gregarious

Light:	bright indirect light
Water:	water consistently, keeping soil moist
Soil:	light, fast-draining soil
Food:	fertilize weekly in spring and summer
Pot:	underpot, repotting every two to three years

Goldfish, prized possessions of ancient Chinese emperors, make a deceptively high-maintenance pet, always complaining about water quality and tank size.

Goldfish *plants*, however, will be only too delighted to share your home, and they are significantly less needy. Same gulping golden charm, completely different attitude, and very likely to become your own prized possession, imperial or not.

Goldfish plants are named for the unexpected look of their flowers—brilliant orange with fused petals that form a bulbous shape with an open "mouth," lending it the resemblance to its namesake. These make wonderful hanging plants, with stems of small green leaves and orange flowers cascading down from a pot.

A tropical plant native to Brazil, goldfish plants look to you to create a similarly humid, moist, warm environment in your home. This would be an ideal plant for a bathroom or kitchen or in proximity to other houseplants—placement that would lend sultriness to the air—though you can also create that ambience with a tray of wet pebbles evaporating near your goldfish plant.

Water often enough to keep the soil from drying out in between. Some gardening experts suggest cutting back on watering during the winter months to encourage spring blooms, and certainly most plants need less water during seasons of lower light and less growth.

But as is true with many plants, even those that, like the goldfish plant, like soil on the damp side, overwatering is the quickest way to kill it.

> **Drooping, wilting, yellow, or dropping leaves** are a clue that this plant has been overwatered. When you water, make sure water is draining completely out of the drainage holes. If it's sitting in a saucer, empty the saucer, too. A plant that sits in water or sodden soil will start to rot from the roots up. Feel the soil before watering, and if it still feels wet, wait awhile.
>
> Of course, the goldfish plant will also wilt when it's too dry. Again, test the soil. If it's dry, get it some water right away!

> When you water, be careful to keep water off the leaves. Water drops on the leaves can cause **brown spots**. Carefully water the base of the plant, keeping any moisture in the soil, not on the plant. Similarly, when trying to increase the humidity around your plant, you shouldn't mist it.

> **Legginess,** those stretched-out stems with few leaves, usually means this goldfish could use some more light. Get it closer to a light source, and then

you can trim back scraggly stems to encourage a bushier, leafier, flowery look.

You love your goldfish plant for its flowers, of course. So what do you do **when it stops flowering**? First of all, don't expect year-round performance. Everyone needs a break between periods of brilliance. In a goldfish plant, this is called a dormant period. You would call it a nap. Give it a few weeks, underwater a little, and maybe even shift it to a cooler location. When you move it back into its regular routine, you may find it ready to flower again.

Underpotting also encourages more "fish" per plant, as the goldfish plant likes to be rootbound, sitting snug in its pot.

Goldfish plants come in a variety of colors and patterns, each more brilliant than the last. While it is a plant that requires some attention to detail, it's not nearly as demanding as its fishier namesake. And unlike that namesake, which sooner or later ends up . . . well, flushed, the goldfish plant can live a long time.

Ivy

Hedera helix

Light: bright medium light

Water: water consistently, keeping soil moist

Soil: peaty, fast-draining soil

Food: fertilize monthly in spring and summer

Pot: repot annually

Unless you happen to live in a prestigious northeastern college of venerable age, ivy is likely to be considered an invasive species for your outdoor garden, twining around everything it sees, digging its little clawed vines into every surface. And yet when grown as an indoor plant, ivy is notoriously hard to maintain. What's the opposite of *invasive*?

Dealing with a split personality like this as a houseplant requires a commitment. Ivy (also known as English ivy, to differentiate from other plants of similar name) will demand specific growing conditions, but if you are attentive to its needs, its dark green, pointed, heart-shaped leaves can climb trellises or trail down shelves to add the mystery and enchantment of ancient, forgotten places and ancient, forgotten gods to your humble abode.

Unlike many houseplants that hail from tropical climates, ivy craves cooler temperatures. Something between 50 to 70 degrees is just right for ivy, though that can be a little chilly for a comfortable home. Avoid placing it in naturally warmer areas, like a bathroom or a kitchen, and instead select a room where the temperature tends to be lower, especially at night.

Cool shouldn't mean dark and shady, however. Ivy does need bright (though indirect) light to grow. Cool also doesn't mean dry—ivy likes humidity! It gets humidity naturally outside from the evaporating damp loams and other plants to which it clings. Inside, it would like some regular misting, please. It likes damp soil inside as well. Water often enough that it doesn't dry out beyond the top inch of soil.

When ivy goes wrong, it looks particularly unattractive, as it can be difficult to separate individual dead or ugly leaves from its overall look. So be on the alert for:

Brown, dry-edged leaves mean that you are probably providing too much water for even the moisture-loving ivy. Is the pot draining thoroughly when you add water? (Remember to empty saucers to avoid sitting water!) Are you waiting to water again until the top inch of soil is dry? When ivy's roots are resting in soggy soil, they will rot and no longer provide water or nutrients to the leaves.

Wilted leaves or leaves dropping off can also be signs of overwatering, but they can also be signs that you've added too much fertilizer. Despite its connections to the Greek god of excess, Dionysus, ivy doesn't want too much of a good thing. Fertilize only during the spring and summer growing months, and just once a month even then. If you have overfertilized, rinse the soil well with a thorough watering until water flows through the drainage holes.

Poor growth, scraggly leafless growth, or on ivy varieties that have patterns on the leaves, fading leaf variegation—these mean your ivy yearns for the sun. While direct sun is just too hot and burns the leaves, ivy still craves bright light! A window or even several hours of artificial light will encourage it to reach its full, leafy potential.

When English ivy is unhappy, it's not just less attractive, it's actually at risk. Unhappy plants are a target for predatory household pests. Watch for aphids and spider mites especially, and quickly prune affected leaves. It's also a good idea to follow up by treating the entire plant with neem oil to prevent pests from spreading.

If you've sorted out all of ivy's concerns, you can focus on its look. Do you want it to climb? Provide a trellis and you can prune and shape the ivy into a vertical masterpiece. Prefer a trailing curtain of vine, suggesting a secret garden hidden behind it? Place it on a high shelf and let it climb down.

Jade

Crassula ovata

Light: bright indirect light

Water: water when soil is dry

Soil: succulent mix, fast-draining soil

Food: fertilize quarterly in warmer months

Pot: repot to refresh soil

The money plant, the lucky plant, the friendship tree—whatever you want to call it, the jade plant has earned its reputation as a popular symbol of good luck and good fortune. Easy to grow, easy to propagate, and easy on the eyes, it has made a well-wishing gift to many a new home and business over the centuries since it migrated from its African homeland.

Jade is a name it has earned, with its fleshy oval green leaves reminiscent of the precious mineral. The leaves branch from a trunk-like stem that, as the jade plant matures, looks like the finely drawn trees of a Japanese painting. New leaves appear in pairs, sometimes with a reddish tint to their edges. Jade is a succulent, so its pot and soil need to drain well. Water it thoroughly; drain it thoroughly. Even if you're over-eager by nature on the water, resist and don't water again until the soil is dried out.

While not too demanding on water, it does need lots of sun, even occasionally direct sun, for at least six hours a day. It won't need to be repotted often, as it grows slowly (and its roots are comfortable being a little snug in the pot), but refresh the soil every few years.

vibrant green leaves =
healthy

limp leaves =
needs water

yellow leaves =
too much water

brown mold on leaves/
white mold on soil =
excess humidity

The jade plant is not one of those head-scratcher plants. It communicates its concerns with refreshing clarity.

Limp leaves. Succulent leaves should look . . . well, succulent: plump and bursting with green juices. If the leaves are looking a little floppy, it's time to get watering. Remember to add water until it flows from the pot's drainage holes. But the jade plant does favor drying out between showers, so limp leaves are a signal, not a disaster.

Yellowing leaves. Oops, overdid it on the watering, didn't you? Your jade plant is too wet and starting to rot from the roots up. Check that the pot has good drainage. Check that there is no sitting water in the pot's saucer. Check that the soil you've used is a light cactus or succulent mix that drains well. Then stop watering so often. Wait until the soil is dry before adding more water. A yellowing jade plant can usually be revived if you give it a chance to dry out.

Dropping leaves. You may also observe unusually small leaves and leggy, leafless growth. Your jade plant is striving for more sunshine. It will want light exposure for at least six hours a day, so find a bright corner for it to revive and replenish.

Brown patches. Okay, but not such a bright corner that it gets a sunburn! Jade leaves won't enjoy direct hot sun and will burn quickly. Indirect light is best. If it does get some direct sun, limit the hours of exposure, and preferably place it near an east-facing window.

Black mold on the leaves or white mold on the soil. Overwatering is probably a factor here, but excess humidity is also playing a part. Get good air circulation around your plant, moving it away from clusters of other, damper plants. Wipe the mold off and replace the soil and pot.

Pests. These guys are not a big problem for jades, but you may sometimes see mealybugs if your plant has been stressed or exposed to other infested plants. Wipe the leaves down with a cotton ball dipped in alcohol until you get rid of unwanted visitors.

No flowers. While jade plants can produce tiny white starlike flowers, it's rare to see them on indoor plants. Just love your jade plant for itself.

If you really have no luck with keeping your jade plant alive, you can always start over. Select a healthy green leaf, snap it off gently, and set it on top of some fresh potting soil. It won't be long before it starts to produce tiny new leaves and roots—a brand-new jade plant! Good luck, and this time, don't overwater!

JASMINE

Light: bright light, indirect with some direct
Water: water consistently, keeping soil moist
Soil: peaty, fast-draining soil
Food: fertilize monthly in spring and summer
Pot: repot as needed, refresh soil annually

Climbing, twining, and trailing long vines with dark green glossy leaves and scattered with tiny star-shaped white blossoms, jasmine can intoxicate your indoor garden with a rewarding, sensuous beauty. When it blooms, jasmine produces a heady, almost indecent perfume that is particularly sweet at night.

There are several varieties of jasmine that do well indoors, but they grow differently, so pick one that fits what you're looking for. Climbing varieties have an appealing look—*Jasminum polyanthum* and star jasmine are good bets—but if your space and style are not suited to vines, there are shrub jasmine plants as well (such as orange jasmine). Not all jasmine produces scented blooms either, so if aroma is your goal, choose wisely. Both star jasmine and orange jasmine are particularly smelly.

Jasmine looks to the light, and lots of it. This plant grows fast when it sunbathes, and even enjoys up to four hours of direct light daily. It prefers damp soil at all times—that's damp, not soaked, so give it good drainage. It will grow fast in the growing season, but resist the urge to prune too much until after it has finished blooming. Jasmine blooms in the late winter months; support its flowering with a nitrogen-light fertilizer and a snug pot.

Overwatering, underwatering, and all the usual houseplant common complaints certainly require appropriate attention from jasmine fanciers, but the biggest worry that haunts a jasmine grower is more specific: Why isn't my jasmine blooming?

That's why you wanted a jasmine plant, after all—for its delicate flowers and enchanting odor. Otherwise, it's just another houseplant with rather leggy vines and small leaves.

What to do when your jasmine refuses to bloom:

Take its temperature. Jasmine likes to chill at night, so find it a location where the temperature dips during dark hours. This is not a radiator plant. Some jasmine enthusiasts even like to move their plant outside during spring and fall so the plant can take advantage of colder evenings. Just don't let it get colder than 40 to 50 degrees.

Is it eating well? Jasmine isn't looking for a big fertilizer meal. Use too much plant food and it may just decide not to bloom. Dilute the fertilizer before feeding your jasmine, and don't add it more than once a month (and only in spring and summer). Pick a solution that has little to no nitrogen in it.

Tuck it in well. Jasmine will bloom more if it is slightly rootbound, meaning its roots are snug in the pot. Give it a big pot and it will put its energy toward growing roots, not flowers. Repot only when roots are actually growing out of the pot, and then expect it to skip blooming for a while.

Dampen its brow. Well, let's dampen its roots instead. If the soil dries up, so does the flower. Keep it moist (not soggy!) when in bloom. If it gets too wet, the roots will rot and flowers will wither and die. If it gets too dry, leaves and buds will start to turn brown and dry.

Lighten up. Jasmine craves sun. Four hours of direct sun a day plus plenty of indirect sun will keep it blooming happily. But don't bake it in the greenhouse effect of a hot window—remember that it still likes to cool off at night.

Prune prudently. Buds emerge from new growth, so if you have clipped back every new shoot in an aggressively controlling attempt at pruning, you will not get flowers. Give it space to grow, let it bloom, and trim it for shape, not to eliminate all new growth.

Respect the natural life span. Jasmine flowers will not last forever. This is not a long-blooming orchid or bromeliad. Each bud will burst into a white to slightly pink, star-shaped, fragrant flower, and then brown and dry up after a few days. What keeps a jasmine plant sweet-smelling for so long is not each individual bud, but the sheer volume of flowers it produces over many weeks.

Jasmine's habit in northern climes is to bloom indoors in the late winter to early spring, often starting in February. It is sweetest at night, giving the dark hours of your late-winter doldrums a hint of the new year of growth to come.

KALANCHOE

Light: bright indirect light

Water: water when soil is dry, drain well

Soil: fast-draining mix of cactus or succulent soil and regular potting soil

Food: fertilize monthly in spring and summer

Pot: repot every two years, good drainage

This may be the ideal plant: good-looking *and* has a good personality.

It is as rare to find this combination in the plant world as it is on a dating app, but kalanchoe is that unusual houseplant that features both gorgeous flowers and a low-maintenance care regimen.

Unlike many tropical succulents with similar growing needs, this Madagascar native is prized for its blooms. Its flowers come in an array of white, yellow, pink, orange, and red, and are arranged in tiny bouquets clustered atop long green stems that emerge from among its shiny, scalloped-edge green leaves. Kalanchoe can flower repeatedly through most of the year, making it a constant source of color and interest in your home.

In common with other succulents, kalanchoe does best with a hands-off approach. Stick to the succulent rule of plant ownership: Just say something nice and keep walking. Kalanchoe likes to dry out between showers, so start by installing it in a pot with good drainage (must have drainage holes in the bottom!), filled with soil that drains quickly, without retaining too much water. A cactus or succulent mix, perhaps combined with a regular potting soil, will do well here. When you do water the plant, water with enthusiasm. No dribbling tablespoons of fluid—give it a good washdown, with water flowing out through its drainage holes. Then let the soil dry out before you water again, sometimes waiting as long as a month.

Kalanchoe doesn't need to be repotted often, as it doesn't grow quickly. Select a pot that fits the root ball, with perhaps an inch of growing space. A pot that is much too large will retain too much water (and you know your kalanchoe doesn't like to be wet).

Not such a hard routine to follow, is it? Nevertheless, there are a few things you can do to upset the easygoing kalanchoe:

Overwater. Kalanchoe should never be mushy. If you see soft, flabby leaves turning to mush, changing to a lighter, almost translucent green, and even falling off the stems, this plant has probably been overwatered. Let it dry out. *Really* dry. Cut away the mushy parts that are caused by rotting roots. If the plant is too damaged and past recovery, select a remaining healthy sprig or leaf and propagate a new one!

Underwater. This mistake is easier to correct. Yes, underwatered leaves can also be described as wilted and floppy, similar to those of an overwatered plant, but leaves that are too dry will also get a wrinkled look, shriveling up and turning brown at the edges. The solution is clear: Water the plant.

Too much sun. Brown patches on the leaves, sometimes looking dry and cracked, mean that the plant is scorching in the sun. This is a sunburn! Kalanchoe won't enjoy direct sun, and a burned leaf will not recover. Remove unsightly leaves and be more cautious about sunshine.

Not enough sun. At the other extreme, a kalanchoe that isn't getting enough light will start to stretch out, growing long, thin stems in a desperate attempt to get closer to the sun. Left like this, the stems will eventually become too long to sustain the growth and will collapse. Move this plant to a brighter spot.

Too much fertilizer. Fertilize the kalanchoe with caution, as it doesn't need much in the way of plant food and will pop out in brown spots on its leaves if you overfertilize. If you see white deposits building up on the soil or see those spots on the leaves, cut out fertilizing for a while and give your plant a thorough watering to rinse chemical deposits from the soil. Avoid fertilizing during the winter months altogether.

Pests. The healthier you keep your kalanchoe, the less likely it is to attract pests. But if you do spot creepy-crawlies on your kalanchoe, attack immediately before they spread. Aphids can be washed away with water. Mealybugs should be wiped off with a cotton swab dipped in rubbing alcohol. Scale insects or more aggressive infestations should be treated with an insecticide.

And finally, you ask, what should you do about dead flowers on your otherwise gorgeous kalanchoe? Hey, dead flowers are normal! You didn't do anything wrong. The flowers bloom, you enjoy them, and then they fade and dry. Prune dead flowers to encourage new ones to grow . . . because no one likes to look at dead flowers, especially on a plant that is as comfortable a companion as the kalanchoe.

Lavender

Lavandula

Light: bright light, three to four hours direct sun
Water: water when top inch of soil is dry
Soil: fast-draining alkaline potting mix
Food: fertilize twice a year, spring and fall
Pot: repot annually in early spring

A summer's day in Provence—fields of lavender spread out before you, the floral, piney scent heavy in the hot sunshine . . . or, since France is a pretty extensive trip for a weekday, set a pot of lavender on your windowsill and let the aroma transport you for free.

Your lavender plant will likely be dreaming of French farmland as well, so much so that trying to get your home environment to imitate the sunny, arid climates (where lavender thrives outdoors) is the key to keeping your houseplant happy.

Sunshine (and lots of it) is the secret to success for an indoor lavender bush. Here's a plant that actually likes direct sun! Find a south-facing window that will afford it at least three to four hours of intense hot light a day. It craves light so much that you may want to periodically rotate the pot so that its stems don't grow bent toward the light source.

Lavender is not too demanding on hydration (it likes a little drought), so water only when the soil is dry, and make sure you keep the water off its perfumed leaves. Dampness is its enemy, so use a soil that will drain quickly, preferably something lightweight and sandy. The pot should give the roots only an inch or two of extra growing space, as its root ball likes to be in more compact settings. A snugger pot will also help it dry out better between waterings.

The scent of lavender is considered soothing, a natural de-stressor. Here's what to watch for to make sure your lavender avoids stress, too:

Few flowers, low growth. You might also notice that the leaves are less fragrant and paler in color. Bring on the sun! Lavender suffers in the shade. Find a warmer, brighter location where the sun's rays hit straight on.

Few flowers, lots of leaf growth. Like many Americans, this lavender is overfed. Lavender really doesn't need much fertilizer, and feeding it too often and too heavily causes it to focus on leaf growth or, in extreme cases, dry and wilted leaves and branches. Fertilize twice a year, in the spring and fall. Adding some alkalinity to the soil by mixing in some crushed limestone while repotting will be more useful to your lavender than extra plant food.

Yellow, wilted leaves. Warning: root rot! Lavender wants fast-draining, dry soil. When the soil is too wet, the roots begin to rot, and the first you may know of it is yellow leaves, especially near the base of the plant. Repot that plant right away, removing as much old soil as possible and cutting away mushy and smelly sections of root and plant. If you're lucky, and you let the plant dry out well, it may recover, but once rot has set in, it can be hard to save. If the plant is past recovery, select a healthy stem cutting and grow a new one!

Black, dry, and brittle leaves. Lavender is susceptible to fungus and mildew, especially if its leaves get wet or its setting is especially still and humid.

When you water, hit the soil, not the leaves. Find a low-humidity location (this houseplant is not a great choice near a shower or bath, for example), separate it from other humidity-producing houseplants, and maybe open a window on a nice day to enjoy the breeze. If your lavender is suffering from a fungus or mildew, cut off and throw away the infected leaves and treat the plant and soil with a fungicide. As is true with root rot, this would be a good time to repot, clearing away old soil and treating your plant to a fresh, clean environment.

Drooping leaves. Good news—this problem is easy to fix. If those limp leaves are accompanied by very dry soil, you are probably underwatering. Just add water.

Pests and diseases. Lavender isn't especially susceptible to pests indoors, but keep an eye out for spittlebugs (foamy substance on leaves), whiteflies (yellowed and dropping leaves), and aphids (dropping and misshapen leaves). Rinse off with water, wiping off more stubborn pests. Aphids can also spread alfalfa mosaic virus, which shows up as bright yellow patches under the leaves. This disease can't be treated, unfortunately, and you will need to say a fond goodbye to this plant.

Because lavender's chief joy is its scent, you will be tempted to save some of its fragrant blossoms to dry and keep. Go for it! But be careful when pruning. Cut away only new growth, not the established woody growth, which can split and die when injudiciously pruned. New flowers will emerge only from new growth!

Lucky Bamboo

Dracaena sanderiana

Light: bright indirect light

Water: one inch of water in the container; if using soil, keep soil moist

Soil: none, pebbles, or fast-draining soil

Food: one drop of fertilizer monthly

Pot: periodically clean algae growth from pot

Ask yourself, do you feel lucky? If you've got a *Dracaena sanderiana,* of course you do! This is a good luck plant, bringing prosperity, health, and happiness. Also, it is ridiculously easy to care for, which is a kind of good fortune in itself.

A bundle of jointed light green stalks crowned with intermittent leaves, lucky bamboo is probably already familiar to you, as it has appeared on many a desk or windowsill in its time, sometimes growing straight or growing manipulated into spirals or woven into interesting shapes. Actually, it's not really bamboo, nor is it from China, where true bamboo has a long-standing reputation for good luck. Lucky bamboo is from Africa and has been trading on its bamboo-ish appearance to get into the good fortune game. If that doesn't help you manifest well-being, what will?

Lucky bamboo earns five stars right up front by being one of the few plants that is hard to kill by overwatering. It lives in water. Set it in a vase or pot and choose your growing medium: soil, pebbles, or water. Soil may be the hardest to maintain, as you will need to make sure it drains well and doesn't stay soggy around the plant roots. If you pot it in pebbles or water, however, all you need is to keep an inch or so of clean water covering the roots at all times.

Indirect light, tending toward shade rather than direct sun, will keep your lucky bamboo growing. It will grow toward the light, so rotate it regularly to maintain those straight, sturdy stalks. Trim excessive leaves and offshoots back if it's getting too bushy or top-heavy.

Lucky bamboo should always have a fresh, bright green color to it. If it starts turning yellow, this is when you need to start paying attention. Yellow leaves can mean:

Sunburn! Dracaenas of many types prefer the dappled light of a tropical forest's understory. Avoid hot sun and hours of direct light. By contrast, if you overreact and move the bamboo to a dark corner, its stem will grow spindly and thin, bending toward any glimpse of light.

Keep it clean! Dirty water sitting around your plant's roots will grow algae, bacteria, and fungus that can harm the plant. Refresh the water once a week. If you are potting it in soil, make sure the pot has good drainage, because while bamboo doesn't mind sitting in water, it can't tolerate sitting in mud. Displaying your luck in a glass vase? That clear glass, allowing in plenty of light, can stimulate algae growth, so consider either an opaque vase or more frequent clean water. If you do see stuff clouding the water, clean the container out with soap and water, gently rinse the plant roots, and get your bamboo set up again with fresh water.

But not too clean. Chemicals in tap water will also yellow your plant's leaves, especially chlorine and fluoride. You can use distilled water or just let water sit out for twenty-four hours for chemical evaporation before adding to your bamboo.

Yellow leaves are mostly curable. However, if the plant's stalk turns yellow, you have a bigger problem. A yellow stalk is a dying stalk. It has likely been badly underwatered or infected by bacteria or fungus in the water. If only one stalk in a cluster is damaged, remove the dead stalk, carefully rinse the remaining stalks, and repot them in a clean pot with clean water.

It is unclear what happens to your luck if your lucky plant dies, but surely the gods of good fortune will smile upon you for diligent plant parenting if you keep trying.

Maidenhair Fern

Adiantum raddianum

Light: bright indirect light

Water: one to two times per week, consistently moist

Soil: well-draining but nutrient-rich soil

Food: not needed

Pot: repot every one to two years, good drainage

Sprightly green petal- or fan-shaped leaves scattered daintily along its fronds make this winsome beauty easy to desire. The maidenhair fern is a love-at-first-sight kind of houseplant. It's not until further into the relationship that you discover just how high-maintenance this princess of the plant world can be.

Its name is not in fact a reference to a hirsute aspect or one's marital status; it borrows its name from the Latin title of a cousin plant, *Adiantum capillus-veneris*, very loosely translated into "unwetted Venus's hair." (Venus was the original maiden, and *unwetted* comes from the way water rolls off the leaves as easily as off a duck's back, as they say.) However, this fern has taken the title and run with it, with a list of delicate needs requiring the patience and commitment of true chivalry.

Humid air, moderate temperatures, damp soil, and partial shade create the right ambience for your fern. It droops without enough humidity and wilts without proper watering. A schedule won't suffice; you'll have to check frequently to see how it's feeling and be prepared to adapt your routine to its preferences.

When unhappy, the maidenhair fern's go-to response is to turn brown or cast aside its leaves. It may not share the reasons for its pique. It's up to you to think about what you've done wrong and make amends.

Is your watering technique inadequate? Ferns like consistently moist soil. They can't stay wet and muddy or the roots will rot, killing the plant from the bottom up. But they also can't dry out. One moment of excessively arid soil and the fern may drop its leaves in disgust. Check the soil frequently to make sure your fern always has not too much and not too little water.

Is your ambience pleasantly tropical? In the wild, ferns live in the damp forest undergrowth, and they want that same humid air and even temperature indoors. Select a more humid location—like a bathroom or near a kitchen sink—to settle your fern. If you live in a particularly dry climate (or it's a dry time of year), you can up the moisture level by giving that fern a spritz of water or keeping the oft-mentioned tray of damp pebbles in its vicinity. Keep temperatures between 65 and 75 degrees, avoiding sharp temperature changes and drafts from AC vents or heaters.

Is the sun's attention too intense? Not used to the harsh gaze of direct light, your maidenhair fern will shrivel in dismay when scorched by bright sun.

Indirect light only, please, but still plenty of it—going to the other extreme of a dark corner will also result in brown, discarded leaves.

Does your fern have enough room to grow? Tight quarters for its roots make for a fussy fern. While a fern doesn't have to be repotted often, when roots start pushing out of drainage holes or emerge from the soil, and when water doesn't seem to wet the soil so much as run right through it, it's time for a new pot. Give those roots a larger space in a (slightly) larger pot.

Have you been force-feeding your fern? Maidenhair ferns don't really need much in the way of fertilizer, and a little becomes way too much very quickly. Fertilize not at all or with caution. Ferns are used to feeding on the slowly rotting plant material of a forest floor, so if you feel compelled to fertilize, use only a slow-release fertilizer or diluted liquid formula. Too much fertilizer burns the roots and—you guessed it—causes it to drop its leaves.

There are more than twelve thousand species of fern in the world, so Mother Nature has clearly identified how to be an effective plant mom for ferns. The maidenhair fern may not be quite as willing to please the indoor parent/gardener, but if you do your best to copy nature's tropical model, this princess of pickiness may yet requite your love.

Money Tree // Guiana Chestnut

Pachira Aquatica

Light: bright indirect light

Water: consistently moist soil

Soil: fast-draining potting mix with peat moss or gravel

Food: diluted fertilizer monthly in spring and summer

Pot: repot to encourage a larger plant, or prune leaves and refresh soil

It's not all about the money, but sometimes it *is* all about the money tree.

While there are several plants nicknamed "money," you can spot this particular plant by its proper name, the Guiana chestnut. It features a leaf pattern probably familiar to you from horse chestnut trees common in American park design. Its shiny leaves are arranged in clusters of six sprouting from each stem. The tree is popularly sold as a group of three or more trunks braided together to create a compact bushy plant that fits nicely on a desk if you keep it pruned or as a large floor plant if you don't. Repotting will encourage it to get bigger fast, so keep the pot small if you favor the diminutive.

Give your money tree a medium amount of light and a well-draining pot because it likes to be watered a lot but can't tolerate staying soaked. Water when the top inch of soil is dry—that soil should be a rich potting soil, but one that drains fast, maybe even a cactus mix. Those lovely shiny leaves ought to be dusted regularly, and misting them during this process gives them a little extra humidity.

This is a hardy plant, but remember: The feng shui financial benefits of a money tree in your home come only from healthy plants. Keep as close an eye on your money tree as Scrooge keeps on his money.

Brown-edged leaves, curled leaves. Get the green back with a little water! If the top inch or so of soil is dry, it's time to water again. Stick to a regular schedule to avoid letting your money tree dry out, though you may need to modify the schedule in winter months.

Yellow leaves, soft stem. Soggy roots turn quickly into a sick plant. Make sure your plant has good drainage. If it drains into a saucer, empty the saucer so the roots aren't sitting in water. If the stem is already soft, quickly repot, removing old, wet soil and any rotten roots to try to save an overwatered money tree.

Brown leaf tips with yellow halos. Improve the atmosphere with a little humidity! A tray of damp pebbles or misting around the plant will help it perk up.

Leggy, few leaves. A stretched-out money tree is looking for the sun, so anxious in its quest for light that it fails to produce bushy leaves. While sitting in direct rays can burn the leaves, brightness matters. Move it out of the shade and into the light. It will fill out again once it's confident in its light (and, thus, food) source.

Pests. Watch out for spider mites—yellow spots on the leaves, and webs and critters under the leaves. Mealybugs and scale can also be a concern. You'll see these easily if you take a moment to examine your money tree investments regularly. Wipe off unwanted guests with an insecticide or a cotton ball dipped in rubbing alcohol.

Dropping leaves. What's the cause? All of the above and then some! Money trees lose leaves when they are stressed. It can be a simple short-term stress, like when you repot or when you move the plant, especially when it first joins your household. But it can also lose leaves when it's overwatered, underwatered, too shady, too sunny, pest infested, or just not in the mood. Don't mourn lost leaves. Get to work identifying its concerns and trust that it will grow new foliage.

And losing leaves can even be intentional. Some Guiana chestnut enthusiasts favor pruning to keep the plant's top fuller and its braided base more striking. Leaves can pop out along the base or the stems. If these leaves are clipped off, the money tree can focus its energy on the crown. But there's also no rule that says you can't have leaves sprouting from different places on the stems. It's your money.

Monstera

Monstera deliciosa

Light: bright indirect light

Water: weekly, drying out soil in between

Soil: peaty potting soil

Food: monthly, or not at all

Pot: repot every two years, good drainage

Some things just get better with age. Fine wine. French cheese. Authors of plant books. And of course the *Monstera deliciosa*.

As a baby, the monstera has solid, heart-shaped leaves. The teenage plant leaves begin to part into fingers. The mature plant leaves add oval perforations between the fingers like a crocheted doily. These lacy tropical beauties grow enthusiastically and only get better-looking as they get older.

A long-term relationship with a *Monstera deliciosa* is rewarding because it is not an overwhelmingly difficult companion to please. It likes to dry out a little between waterings, so it's suited to the forgetful plant parent. It doesn't need frequent repotting or excessive fertilizing. Comfortable with rainforest undergrowth, it will be happy with the indirect light from a window.

Most of monstera's concerns are familiar enough to houseplant owners—too much or too little light, and too much or too little water. Here are the clues to watch for:

Yellow leaves usually mean too much water. Like most houseplants, monstera needs good drainage so that water doesn't collect around the roots but just wets the soil and flows on through. Before you water again, stick your finger into the soil. Are the top one to two inches of soil dry? Then it's time to water! If they're still wet, hold off.

Shiny brown patches mean that the plant has suffered so much from over-watering that root rot has set in. This would be a good time to repot, re-moving soaked soil and cutting away smelly dead root material. Give your monstera a clean home and it may be able to re-cover. Use a soil that is peaty, but not packed so densely that it can't drain well. Make sure there's enough room for roots to grow (an inch or two larger than the previous pot). If you're having trouble getting the plant to dry out enough for fresh water each week, consider moving it to a brighter, warmer location to help evaporate extra moisture from the soil.

Crispy brown edges on the leaves usually occur when the monstera is feel-ing a little dehydrated. Did you forget to water? Check whether the soil is dry and get back into the routine of regular watering! The edges won't turn green again, but the plant will recover quickly.

Drooping leaves can happen both when your monstera is underwatered or overwatered, so this will be a time you'll have to check the soil carefully and pay attention to other clues. Is the soil wet and maybe a little smelly? Over-watered. Is the soil parched dry? Underwatered.

Brown spots with a yellow circle around them are signs of a fungus. Cut away the damaged leaves and avoid splashing the leaves when you water. Fungal growth often starts when the plant is getting overwatered, so consider cutting back and giving your plant a chance to dry out a little. If the fungus recurs, it's a good time to move to a clean new pot with clean new soil.

Slow growth can mean your monstera isn't getting its full daily dose of sunshine. While it will burn in direct rays, it still needs lots of bright light. Keep it closer to a window, especially an east- or west-facing window that gives good light without creating too much heat.

Lack of light can also prevent the leaves from splitting into the characteristic monstera lace doily look. However, before you panic and force your plant to sunbathe, do you know how old it is? Monstera leaves won't split while the plant is young, and it takes as many as two to three years for the monstera to reach that level of maturity. Take care of your monstera, and it will get there! This is a long-term relationship, one that gets more rewarding as the years go by.

For such a pleasant and reliable houseplant, it's unfortunate that the monstera is subjected to so much name-calling. Some people have nicknamed it the split-leaf philodendron or the swiss cheese plant, which is odd, since it is neither of these plants. Stick with its proper name, *Monstera deliciosa*, named for the fragrant fruit it grows in the wild (but rarely produces indoors), which also earns it another unique nickname: the fruit-salad plant.

Norfolk Island Pine

Araucaria heterophylla

Light: full sun
Water: consistently moist
Soil: peaty, sandy, acidic potting soil
Food: use a diluted fertilizer regularly
Pot: repot every one to two years

With so many houseplants these days going for that tropical vibe, the Norfolk Island pine is a refreshing change—like a living Christmas tree, its needled branches and triangular aspect lend a wintry breath of northern style to your home.

But in fact the Norfolk Island pine is fooling you. Not only is it *not* a pine tree, but it comes from the South Pacific. This doesn't really matter if you love how it looks, but it does matter when it comes to managing its needs. You'll need to think *subtropical* instead of *mountain forest.* It needs humidity. It needs moisture. It needs sunlight. It needs attention more of the year than just during the winter solstice celebrations.

Start with the right conditions. This plant craves full sun and lots of it—no dark corners and shady nooks! A bright window or doorway will be a better choice.

All of that sun does encourage evaporation, so you may need to monitor moisture levels—water and air—around your Norfolk Island pine more closely than you would other houseplants. Its soil should stay consistently moist. Poke a finger in the pot. Are the top two inches dry? Time to water. Water thoroughly, letting water flow through drainage holes. If it's sitting in a saucer, empty water out of the saucer when you're done watering. If your air is dry, mist the plant regularly, or consider placing a tray of wet pebbles under or near your pine.

A young plant grows slowly, so it will not need to be repotted more than once every two years, or even less frequently. If you keep it for many years, however, it will grow more vigorously—and require more pruning—as it ages. To really stunt its growth, you can prune the central stalk or trunk. However, it then loses its Christmassy shape, so save this as a last resort for when it threatens to outgrow your home!

A Norfolk Island pine will keep you on your toes! Here are some problems to watch for:

Yellow needles. You may think of arid western slopes when you're looking at your pine, but it's thinking about more water. A Norfolk Island pine won't put up with occasional dribbles of water or tolerate outright neglect. Water well. Then water again before it dries out.

Brown needles. There may be more than a pine living in your house. Check your plant for pests, looking carefully among needles, where those mealybugs, aphids, or whiteflies like to hide. If you find any unwanted guests, spray with insecticidal soap. Repeat until your plant is clean and green again.

Dropping branches and needles. While this Norfolk Islander likes moist soil, it doesn't like soggy soil. If water is not draining well and pooling around the roots (or if you just water too often so the soil never has a chance to dry), it can cause root rot. As the roots die, the plant will, too. Let it dry out and repot. Pursue a less rigorous watering schedule in the future.

Leggy growth. No one wants a scraggly pine. This plant is starving for sunshine. Move it to a brighter location and cut back on fertilizer for a few weeks so it can even out its growth. Since this is a sun-loving plant, you may want to rotate it periodically so it doesn't start to lean toward the light.

A few yellow or brown needles or dropped branches are normal as the plant grows, especially among its lower branches. When you need to get concerned is when unhealthy needles or branches start appearing all over the plant. After you've found your plant parenting mistake—too much water, too little, etc.—be sure to prune away dead or damaged branches. Not only are they less than lovely, but your plant doesn't need or want them anymore. And now that your Norfolk Island pine is pretty again, feel free to decorate it for Christmas! Even if it's July!

Orchid

Orchidaceae

Light: bright indirect light

Water: weekly, or when completely dry

Soil: orchid mix or moss

Food: orchid fertilizer before and after blooming

Pot: repot when roots are pushing through the container

An orchid is a paradox of a plant. Weeks of showy beauty followed by months of spartan plainness. Simple needs but very specific needs. Moisture without wetness. Potting soil without soil. Orchid relationships require patience and fortitude . . . but the feeling of accomplishment you get when, after a year of careful tending, that dazzling bloom emerges is hard to top.

The key to orchid success is ritual. Develop routine habits around your orchid care and these houseplants become remarkably easy to maintain.

1. Bright light without direct sun. An east- or west-facing window would be ideal.
2. Pot selection dictates the growing medium. If you are using a solid pot (with good drainage holes!), use an orchid mix that contains a lot of bark. If you are using an open-work basket, use a sphagnum moss to provide a good base.

3. Water only once a week so that the growing medium can dry out completely in between showers. When you do water, take your time, making sure the bark or moss has a chance to get wet.

4. If you live in a dry environment or it's a dry time of year, add in some humidity with a tray of wet pebbles under or near your orchid. Just make sure your plant's roots aren't resting in any moisture.

5. Fertilize twice a year, once before it blooms and once after. Blooming is hungry work.

6. You will feel confident and successful while your orchid is in bloom, those splendid flowers showing up like an award for your hard work. It is harder to be certain of your plant parenting skills when all you are caring for are a few waxy leaves and a tangle of thick roots. Stick with your routine. If you keep up with the good habits you developed while it was blooming, you can manage through the slow months until it blooms again. Here are the problem points to keep an eye on:

Tan dry patches on the leaves. Too much sunlight for an orchid's taste. The direct rays can burn its leaves. Move it into indirect light. While the sunburned patches will not recover, the leaves can continue to grow. Wait to cut off damaged leaves until new ones have grown to keep your plant healthy.

Darkening leaves. This orchid needs brighter light. Leaves sometimes darken on a plant that's not getting enough sunshine, and too little light can also cause flower buds to fall off before blooming. Remember to dust off or shower the leaves periodically, too, so light is making its way to the leaf's chlorophyll!

ORCHIDS

Dendrobium
Orchid

Moth Orchid

Cattleya Orchid

Yellow, floppy leaves or black roots. An orchid's roots should be a plump greenish gray. If they're turning black and mushy, your orchid is experiencing root rot, caused by overwatering. As the roots rot, the leaves will jaundice and turn flabby. An orchid should never have water pooling in its pot and around its roots. Lift the orchid from its pot and remove any dead roots. Repot in a clean pot with new potting material and let it dry out to revive. If the rot has spread up into the crown of the plant, it will not recover. But hopefully you won't let it get this far! Just make sure the pot is draining well and that you hold off on watering until the orchid potting material is completely dry.

Roots filing the entire pot. Orchids grow roots with energy, and over time they'll completely fill a pot. If you have a slatted basket, roots will grow right out of the slats! This is normal and healthy, but when a pot is filled with roots, move it to a larger container with fresh potting material so it can keep on growing.

Yellow spots on the leaves. Pest control! Mealybugs, spider mites, scale, and other pests will leave dead spots on the leaves when they take a bite. Spray the leaves with an insecticidal soap regularly until your unwanted guests are gone.

Black spots on the leaves. There's a fungus among us. Spray the plant thoroughly with neem oil to kill the fungus, but also take a moment to think about why a fungus might grow. Are you watering too often, keeping your orchid too wet? Is there good air circulation around it?

While these general guidelines apply to most orchids, because there are numerous—too many to list here—orchid varieties, you may need to modify your approach depending on which kind of orchid is letting you share its home. Here are a few popular favorites to love:

- Moth orchids (*Phalaenopsis*) have big, wing-petaled blooms in brilliant purples, pinks, and whites, so perfect in appearance that they are often copied in fake decor.
- You've surely seen *Dendrobium* with sprays of vivid flowers. There's a purple dendrobium floating in your mai tai and definitely one or two on your Hawaiian lei.
- *Cattleya* are ruffled. Some varieties even offer a lovely fragrance!

Orchid growers tend to turn into orchid enthusiasts remarkably quickly. If you've successfully cared for one orchid, prepare yourself to crave more.

Peace Lily

Spathiphyllum

Light: medium to bright indirect light
Water: consistently moist, water weekly
Soil: rich, peaty potting mix
Food: diluted solution monthly in spring and summer
Pot: keep slightly rootbound, good drainage

Finally, a flowering plant to make you feel like an accomplished houseplant owner without really any more effort than any of the tropical vines require. This is a year-round companion to breathe fresh air into even your dark winter months—literally. The peace lily is one of those on NASA's list of air-purifying plants, making each deep breath a more peaceful experience.

The peace lily produces a dense cluster of dark green shiny oval leaves and can grow up to three or four feet tall. Thus it can be used as a floor plant or kept smaller on tables and desks. It produces long-lasting white flowers consisting of a hoodlike sheath offsetting an off-white center stalk.

It's a rainforest native, hailing originally from tropical regions around the equator, so your job as a peace lily parent is to replicate those temperate conditions in your home. Water regularly (usually weekly) to keep its soil damp at all times—but never soggy and wet. A medium amount of light and a good wipe-off to remove dust periodically will keep it happy. It doesn't care for a lot of fertilizing and it likes to be somewhat rootbound, sitting snug in its pot, so you won't have to plan on frequent repotting. Add some humidity during dry, hot months and avoid big temperature fluctuations (don't set it near an AC vent or heater).

Peace lilies are good communicators, so when problems do arise, they can be quickly addressed.

Drooping, wilting leaves. Time to water! Those leaves will perk right back up after a good drink. If you remain careless about watering, over time your lily will start to show dry brown leaf tips and edges.

If you keep seeing brown tips, consider letting tap water sit out for twenty-four hours before giving it to your lily. Peace lilies are a bit sensitive to chlorine in the water.

Wilted, yellowing leaves. Yes, this can look similar to an underwatered plant, but these yellowing leaves suggest overwatering instead. Is the soil already wet, maybe even soggy? Overwatered. Poke the soil a little. Are the roots mushy and smelly? Very overwatered. A peace lily's soil should never be a muddy mess. Get a pot with drainage holes. If the pot has a saucer, empty the saucer of overflow water after watering so the plant doesn't sit in a pool. To rescue an overwatered peace lily, start by repotting in a snug, clean pot with fresh potting mix. Give it a chance to dry out more between waterings—wait until the top inch of soil is dry before adding more water!

Yellow leaves. If your watering technique is right but your leaves are still yellow, maybe your peace lily is looking for a little light? While the peace lily is known for handling lower light conditions well, it still needs some brightness. Indirect light from an east-facing window is ideal.

yellow, wilted leaves =
overwatered

no flowers =
needs more light or
to be repotted

brown spots or streaks =
too much direct sun

drooping leaves =
needs water

Brown spots or streaks on the leaves. Of course, as with many tropical plants, blazing direct sunshine will just cause a sunburn, characterized by brown patches. Cut away damaged leaves and move it out of the glare.

Brown edges. Peace lilies can be sensitive to aggressive fertilizing, so if your watering technique is consistent and you're still seeing brown edges on the leaves, you might be feeding it too much. Always use a diluted solution and never fertilize in the winter. To recover, water thoroughly until excess water is flowing through drainage holes, rinsing out fertilizer buildup in the soil.

Brown tips. Tropical plants love humidity. Give it a little mist if it's looking brown on the tips. Grouping it with other plants or setting it on a tray of wet pebbles also adds more moisture to the air.

No flowers. You loved this lily for its bloom, right? Peace lilies will withhold flowers if they don't get enough light. Find a brighter spot. Peace lilies can also stop blooming if they haven't been repotted in a few years. Get it some fresh soil!

There are lots of types of peace lilies, so you can pick the mature plant size and look that suits you, from the 'Power Petite' variety to the strikingly named 'Mauna Loa Supreme'. This is an easygoing houseplant, so feel confident about your ability to grow it successfully. Then sit back, breathe the purified air it produces, and feel at peace.

Peperomia

Light: bright indirect light

Water: every one to two weeks, when top few inches of soil are dry

Soil: well-draining potting mix or orchid mix

Food: diluted fertilizer monthly or none

Pot: repot every two to three years

No, peperomia is not a pizza topping. It's an epiphytic South American rainforest transplant that's having a bit of a moment as a houseplant. Sometimes called a baby rubber plant (though it is not in fact at all related to the rubber plant), it is more of a tabletop or shelf plant in size, giving it its other nickname: "radiator plant."

The thousands of varieties of peperomia feature thick, fleshy leaves with interesting textures and dramatic colors like red, green, silver, or purple. Some leaves are big, some are small—you pick which is just right for you.

Whatever style you select, your peperomia comes with a very simple care list. As an epiphyte, it doesn't need heavy, rich soil. Plant it in something that drains fast; some experts even recommend using an orchid potting mix. Water it only when the top few inches of soil are dry, meaning that if you forget occasionally, it will be just fine! It needs that bright indirect lighting typical of rainforest dwellers and only rarely needs fertilizing. It prefers to be rootbound. Repot when roots start growing out of drainage holes, but otherwise, let it snuggle in.

Don't overlook its simple requests just because it's small! Pay attention to:

Yellow leaves. Especially if you spot these near the plant's base, overwatering is the most likely culprit. Is the soil wet? Then your peperomia does not need to be watered. Let it dry out and make sure its pot and soil are draining well. If it gets to the point where leaves are falling off and the stems are mushy, repot with fresh soil and a clean pot. Remove any rotten leaves, stems, and roots!

Limp, drooping leaves. Is the soil dry? Water, please! Give it a good drink, draining thoroughly. Keep a closer eye on when the soil is drying out in the future. If you repeatedly underwater, you can expect dry, curling leaves or brown leaves. If you live in a very dry location, increase the humidity around your plant with a tray of damp pebbles, but most climates don't require extra moisture for peperomia's atmosphere.

Gray-brown or curled leaves. That's a lot of sun for a little peperomia, isn't it? Move it out of direct rays to avoid scorched leaves.

Lack of growth. This is a small plant, but it still should be producing new leaves. It needs more sun! Too much shade can also cause the leaf colors to fade. It also makes it harder for the plant to dry out properly in between waterings.

Pests! Mealybugs, spider mites, whiteflies—if you spot unwanted guests on your plant, treat it with an insecticidal soap. Remember, a happy plant is less likely to get infested!

Peperomia generates a lot of disagreement among indoor gardening experts. Some argue for humid conditions; some warn against them. Some suggest keeping soil moist; others prefer to let soil dry out. Some want a potting soil; others favor a soilless mix. How is a peperomia lover to sort it out? Some of your decisions will be based on the variety you select and some on your personal preferences. Take some time figuring out what your particular peperomia likes.

One thing everyone agrees on—overwatering is the quickest way to end your peperomia relationship. Keep soggy soil away from peperomia roots and you can safely experiment with the rest of your care plan.

Philodendron

Light: bright indirect light

Water: water when the top inch of soil is dry

Soil: well-drained potting mix

Food: monthly in spring and summer

Pot: repot or replace soil every two years

Heart-shaped leaves on a delicate vine trailing and twining around your home in an untamed jungle look: Who wouldn't love a philodendron? It's right there in the name, derived from the Greek words for "love" and "tree."

Your average garden store is most likely to offer the vine variety of philodendron, but there is a plethora of philodendron possibilities should you decide to explore. Some are large, with leaves more than a foot long. Some are bushy, with a crown of green leaves spilling out of the pot. Even the vining type comes with many options—glossy dark green leaves, multicolored leaves, lime-green leaves, large leaves, small leaves, and so on.

Care for all varieties of philodendron is similar, however, and common to many popular tropical houseplants. It wants indirect light, as though bright sun were being filtered through taller rainforest trees. It wants consistent moisture, as though from a humid and damp environment. It wants rich soil, as though replenished by decaying plant life all around.

When most people err with philodendrons, their mistakes tend to demonstrate a lack of consistency rather than any specific poor choice.

Limp leaves, curling in and turning brown. Your philodendron is probably not getting enough water. Check the top inch of soil. Dry? Then it's time to water, taking time to thoroughly wet the soil, letting water flow through drainage holes. An occasional sprinkle won't do it. If it has gotten very dry, water repeatedly (maybe in a shower) until the soil rehydrates throughout.

Droopy leaves with brown edges. Along the same lines, humidity is an important companion to watering. In drier weather or climates, mist the leaves once a week.

Yellow leaves. Once plant owners start watering, they sometimes seem to find it hard to stop! An overwatered philodendron will develop root rot and start dying from the roots up until you see yellowing leaves. You need a pot with good drainage to make sure the roots are not sitting in soggy soil. Let the top inch of soil dry out before watering again. If your plant just isn't recovering, repot into clean soil and remove any mushy roots.

PS: A few yellow leaves every now and then, especially near the base of the plant, are nothing to worry about. This is natural and a normal part of aging.

Leggy vines with few leaves. Imagine the vine is stretching out for some sunshine! If a philodendron isn't getting enough sunshine, it grows longer vines and fewer leaves. Find a brighter location for it.

Yellow patches on the leaves. Direct sun, however, is too bright for a philodendron and will burn the leaves. Keep the light bright but indirect.

Small leaves. While philodendrons don't require a ton of fertilizing, they do still get hungry sometimes and may produce smaller leaves when their soil lacks enough nutrients. Refresh the soil, and if it's still struggling, add some fertilizer.

Roots emerging from soil. Time to repot! Find a slightly larger pot and be sure to use a rich, fresh potting mix to replenish its nutrients. But let's differentiate between roots in the soil and aerial roots. The philodendron vine grows thin yellow wispy roots all along its length. These are a normal part of the vine and not a sign to repot.

Pests. Philodendrons aren't especially attractive to houseplant pests like aphids and spider mites, but a stressed-out plant can easily fall in with a bad crowd. Stay on top of the above problems and the pests will stay away.

When you want to spread the love around, the philodendron is ready and willing to propagate. Simply trim a section of stem/vine (around six inches will be satisfactory) and place the end in water, taking care to keep any leaves out of the water. When the stem produces roots in the water, it's time to pot! Now you have enough philodendron to share . . . or to start a new and larger plant family all your own.

POTHOS

EPIPREMNUM AUREUM

Light: bright indirect light

Water: water when soil is dry

Soil: well-drained potting mix

Food: every other month

Pot: repot when rootbound

Pothos is a plant with a little bit of an identity crisis.

Pothos is a genus of flowering, vining tropical plants. There are tons of varieties, though not often found as houseplants. What most stores are selling under this name is actually *Epipremnum aureum*, in a completely different genus. *Epipremnum aureum* is commonly called golden pothos, aka devil's ivy, Ceylon creeper, money plant, etc. It was once an emigrant from Mo'orea in the French Polynesian Society Islands, but it is now a resident of any and all tropical and subtropical ecosystems.

Its name problem derives from exploring botanists' habit of naming plants by observable features, not genetic makeup. But golden pothos got its name well before complex genetic testing was available, so we'll give those old botanists a pass.

But what's in a name anyway? A pothos by any other name is still a lively addition to your home. In fact it is so easy to grow that it has earned a bit of a reputation as an invasive species in tropical climates, where, when planted outside, it can take over a garden and climb up trees, producing leaves as large as dinner plates. Even in more temperate locales, you've probably spotted it filling built-in planters in indoor malls.

Pothos is a vine, with green heart-shaped leaves usually dashed with a little color, yellow or white. When maintained well, it will form a nice bushy plant with trailing vines. It lasts a long time.

This houseplant prefers a little neglect. It likes bright indirect light in the four- to six-hour range, but won't tolerate much direct light. It likes damp but not wet soil, so it needs to dry out well between waterings. Add fertilizer monthly, since potting soil has few nutrients. Dusting is easy—rinse it off in a shower.

For a beginner houseplanter, pothos is helpful because it's such a good communicator. Just learn its language.

Droopy leaves. You wilt a little when you're thirsty, too, don't you? Give this pothos a drink right away! If you leave it drooping and wilting too long, it will start to get dry brown edges on the leaves. If you've just watered and the leaves are still droopy, however, check the pot. Is it completely full of roots? It needs a bigger pot and fresh soil!

Black spots. Like a cursed pirate, this plant is trying to tell you it's getting too much water. Pothos likes to dry out well between waterings. Perpetually damp soil very quickly turns to root rot. Consider waiting until the leaves begin to droop before watering again. To recover from aggressive watering, let your plant dry out. If the soil is very soggy and maybe a little smelly, shift it to a new pot with clean soil.

Pale leaves or lack of variegation. This depends a little on the variety of pothos you've selected, but if those nice green leaves start to fade in color all of a sudden, it probably needs more light. If you have a variegated variety and the pattern disappears, same story: Step into the light. Pothos needs four to six hours of light a day, and indoor fluorescent lighting counts!

Yellow or brown leaves. Two obvious options for this one. Overwatering is one possibility, as mentioned above. The other option is too much sunshine. Direct sun will damage the leaves quickly, so while it needs plenty of light, it doesn't want that light straight up. Indirect light only!

Pruning plays an important role in maintaining your pothos relationship, and you'll have to be confident and direct on this one. If your pothos is looking leggy, prune back its trailing stems and the plant will be bushier and more compact—just cut the vine about a fourth of an inch above a leaf (you can use discarded trimmings to propagate new plants!). If you like a cascading look, try draping vines down a bookshelf. Prune extraneous and secondary stems so those dominant stems can really grow.

There are some fantastic varieties of pothos, so you can match your vine to your style. Try white-and-green-patterned 'Marble Queen' to give your room a classic look, or the outrageous 'Neon' with brilliant chartreuse leaves, or dainty 'Pearls and Jade', almost as pretty as its name.

Pothos is resilient and sturdy. This is a great starter plant because even if you really can't follow directions and your pothos is struggling, it's easy to propagate from a snip of stem so you can start all over again. Read the directions this time.

Prayer Plant
Maranta leuconeura

Light:	bright indirect light
Water:	consistently moist
Soil:	well-draining potting mix
Food:	diluted solution biweekly in spring and summer
Pot:	repot when rootbound, every three to four years

After a day of rigorous plant parenting, you can do no better than to follow the example of the prayer plant and fold your hands to rest when the day is done.

During the daylight hours, the prayer plant's wide, flat leaves show off feathery patterns of dark and light green with red stems and under-leaves for a dramatic appearance; but when the sun sets, the prayer plant's leaves fold up and inward like praying hands (guess how it got its name).

Here's the prayer plant catechism of care:

1. No direct sunshine, but give your prayer plant plenty of light, especially in darker winter months.

2. Soil (preferably acidic) should drain well—no swampy roots.

3. But water frequently, especially during warmer months. You don't want to let the prayer plant completely dry out. Not too wet. Not too dry. *Juuust* right.

4. Mix that water with some diluted fertilizer every couple of weeks during the warmer months.

5. Misting with warm water can give it that humid air it prefers.

This tropical rainforest native, originally from Brazil, is really just praying for its homeland. Replicate that steamy, damp environment and you'll be blessed with a happy maranta. If you have a hard time remembering your prayers, however, here are a few problems you may run into:

Limp leaves. While it's normal for the prayer plant's leaves to rise or fall depending on the time of day, a limp, drooping leaf is a watering problem. Check the top two inches of soil. Is it dry? Then it is time to water! The maranta prefers soil that stays somewhat moist all the time. If you let it dry out completely—to the point when the leaves are starting to curl and brown—soak it with water until the soil rehydrates.

Yellow leaves. Just don't keep it soaking all the time or you will end up with the opposite problem: overwatering. Prayer plants need soil that drains well and should never be left sitting in soggy soil. Overwatering can quickly cause root rot, characterized by yellowing and dropping leaves. It can also lead to fungal infections that appear as yellow spots on the leaves. If your prayer plant is too wet, repot it in fresh soil and remove any drying or damaged leaves.

Curling leaves. Prayer plants can be a little sensitive about chemicals in the water, especially as they build up in the soil over time. Consider watering with distilled water or water that has been left to sit twenty-four hours before being fed to your plant.

Brown, curling leaves. Similarly, too much fertilizing can cause chemicals to build up in the soil and brown the leaf edges. Water thoroughly, letting water flow through drainage holes to clean the soil. And ease up on the fertilizer, especially during winter months.

Dry brown leaves. Prayer plants are tropical! If your climate lacks humidity, mist your prayer plant or rest it on a tray of wet pebbles to enjoy some humid evaporation. Heaters and AC vents are not good for a prayer plant, so select a location with fewer dramatic temperature changes and drafts.

Brown patches or washed-out coloring. This prayer plant is fading in the direct sun. It prefers indirect light, though too little exposure to bright light will stunt its growth. Just keep it out of direct rays.

White powdery substance or brown spots. Those common indoor pests (spider mites and mealybugs) wouldn't mind making your prayer plant a snack. The healthier your prayer plant, the less likely it is to be attacked by bugs. If you do spot unwelcome company, give your plant a good shower to rinse off pests. You can also treat with insecticidal soap if you're still struggling to get rid of them.

Prayer plants do take a little attention to detail and thoughtfulness, but a good day's work of careful watering and proper potting will reward you with a stylish and unique houseplant. And having completed your labors, you, like your prayer plant, can close up your leaves, rest well, and get ready to tackle tomorrow's indoor gardening projects.

Rubber Plant
Ficus Elastica

Light: bright indirect light

Water: weekly, keeping soil consistently moist

Soil: fast-draining cactus mix

Food: diluted fertilizer no more than monthly during spring and summer

Pot: repot annually, or replace soil

For when you've had enough of the fiddle-leaf fig and all its drama: the rubber plant. Big shiny leaves and statuesque shape, but without many of the touchy attitudes of its *Ficus* cousins.

The rubber plant, a tropical import from Southeast Asia, gets its name from the milk-white sap that oozes from its stems when broken. The sap has been used to make rubber—though it is not the usual commercial choice—but it can also be an irritant if you get it on your skin or ingest it. So don't break off rubber plant leaves and eat them. (Or, and we hope more realistically, don't let your pets do so either.)

Ficus elastica cares about two things when it comes to its care: light and water. Keep light bright and consistent. Keep soil moisture consistent. Regular attention is important—don't "bounce" around a lot—but this isn't the kind of temperamental ficus that shatters at the slightest mischance.

Not being finicky is not the same thing as being carefree. If you aren't sticking to your plant care routines, the rubber plant can struggle with:

Yellow leaves, mushy stems. While a rubber plant likes tropical moisture, excessively wet soil will quickly cause its roots to rot. Dead roots can't feed the plant, so it quickly yellows and starts to develop mushy stems. It can be hard for a rubber plant to recover by the time rot has spread to stems, so your goal should be prevention. Water when the top quarter of the soil is dry. Drain thoroughly.

Drooping, curling, or folded leaves. This is not, however, a cactus—you can't let the soil dry out completely. If the plant's leaves start to fold in on themselves, it's time to water! And prepare yourself for some lost leaves, as stress freaks out everyone in the *Ficus* family.

Dry leaf tips or brown spots. The rubber plant likes more than damp soil. It likes damp air, too. Keep up the humidity level with a nearby tray of damp pebbles or mist the leaves.

Small leaves, changes in leaf color. Rubber plants have a rep for doing well in settings with less light. This may be so, but less light doesn't mean dark. The rubber plant can't grow as well in dim interiors. Find it a brighter location! With its big, flat leaves, this houseplant also benefits from good housekeeping, so break out the duster. Gently wipe down each leaf with a damp cloth once a month or so, so light has a clear path to the chlorophyll.

Leggy stems. Stretched-out gaps between leaves can mean your plant is reaching for more light, but they also suggest it may not be thrilled with your less-than-tropical climate. It prefers warmer temperatures (high 60s, low 70s—who wouldn't enjoy that?). Keep it away from AC vents and heaters.

Leaves falling off. Any major changes in life lead to a rubber plant flinging aside some of its leaves. This should not be taken as a tragedy. It is less prone to such displays than its cousins and mostly reacts with leaf drama when it has experienced a sudden change in light. Just brought it home from a bright greenhouse to your dark apartment? Leaf drop. Moved it from a dark corner to a windowsill? Leaf drop. Give it time and patience. It will adjust.

Bacteria, fungus, and pests. Ugh. Here's a quick translation: brown spots with a yellow halo mean bacteria, brown spots with no halo mean fungus, and webs or brown bugs on the leaves mean bug infestation. Poor water management usually accounts for all three, as a healthy plant is less likely to catch a bug. Too much water often leads to bacterial and fungal growth. Dry it out, repot it, and remove the infected leaves. Uneven watering (sometimes too much, sometimes too little) leaves your plant vulnerable to pests like scale and spider mites. Wipe off the intruders with a cotton ball dipped in rubbing alcohol.

A happy rubber plant can grow quite big, with all the statuesque appeal of a fiddle-leaf fig or *Ficus benjamina* but without the fretful drama. As it grows, it may droop or threaten to tip over. Support it with a pole or dowel to keep both plant and houseplant parent standing tall.

Snake Plant
Sansevieria trifasciata or Dracaena trifasciata

Light: full sun to shade

Water: every three to four weeks, when completely dry

Soil: fast-draining, sandy cactus or succulent mix

Food: diluted cactus fertilizer during spring and summer

Pot: good drainage, repot when roots push out of pot

Look, it's not you, it's me, okay? The snake plant could not possibly be clearer about the relationship it wants with you—its leaves are basically large, sharp spears pointedly indicating that you should leave it alone. Keep in mind that it is nicknamed "mother-in-law's tongue." Getting it now?

Snake plants quite literally want you to stop bothering them. This makes them ideal houseplants for beginners and for those who struggle with remembering basic tasks. Forget to water? Fine. Left it in a dark corner? Fine. Its spiky, variegated green leaves, with little serrated points along their edges, lend a spare, sculptural elegance to any space. And they could hardly be easier to maintain.

Water around once a month—dry soil is good. Choose a shady corner or a bright corner—either will work. Just don't mess around with moving it into different lighting once you've picked one. Fertilize rarely or not at all. That's it, really.

Of course even the most low-maintenance of plants is going to need the occasional check-in. Think of it like your neighbor across the hall. You don't need to invite them over for dinner every night. Just say hey and call the police when the newspapers pile up at their door.

Yellow, drooping leaves. This is the number one example of giving your sansevieria too much attention: overwatering. It doesn't need a weekly drink, okay? Wait until the top four inches of soil are dry and *then* add water. When the snake plant's soil gets too wet—whether that's because of a pot with poor drainage, too large a pot that retains too much moisture, or peaty soil, or because you just can't leave it alone—root rot sets in quickly. The roots turn brown, mushy, and smelly, a less-than-charming situation that then results in yellow or brown mushy leaves. By that time, it may be too late to save your plant. Take our word for it and lay off the wet stuff.

If you do find yourself in a soggy situation, repot your plant. Cut away rotten roots and start over with fresh soil in a clean pot. This will help prevent fungal growth, too. A fungus grows well in wet conditions and will show up as white patches or brown spots on your snake plant leaves. Treat the plant with neem oil and remove damaged leaves.

A droopy snake plant might also be ready for a new pot. If it's not too wet, not too shady, and otherwise healthy, check the roots. Are they filling the pot entirely? Time for a bigger pot!

Dull leaves. A healthy snake plant will have perky bright green leaves. A thirsty plant's leaves will start to dull in color and shine, eventually leading to dry, brown tips. Give it a drink! Stick with a watering routine (every three weeks?) to keep it in condition.

Slow growth. Snake plants don't mind shady conditions, but it can mean they grow more slowly. It's okay, but if you want more growth, move it somewhere brighter. Bright indirect light is the ideal setting. If you are transitioning a snake plant from a shady spot to a sunny spot, do it in stages so as not to shock (and damage) the plant with a sudden change in light.

Sansevieria do appreciate a little housekeeping, too. Dust those leaves every few months so that light can readily reach the leaves. Just do it very carefully—a snake plant isn't a cuddler.

Deformed or stunted leaves. While you may be leaving it alone, it sounds like some other unwanted visitors have made your snake plant home. Mealybugs like to infest leaves close to the soil, where they can be hard to spot, sucking away at your plant's juices. Spider mites are another infestation risk. Wipe both away with a cotton ball or cotton swab dipped in rubbing alcohol.

As long as you can handle the strong, silent type, you and your snake plant will do well together. Give it space and it will make your area fabulous.

Spider Plant
Chlorophytum comosum

Light: bright indirect light
Water: consistently moist
Soil: well-draining, loamy potting mix
Food: as needed in spring and summer
Pot: repot every two to three years

Just because you're ubiquitous doesn't mean you're unlovable. Just ask the Kardashians. Or the spider plant. Since their emigration from Africa, spider plants have moved in and established themselves as a houseplant omnipresence. They're pretty in a delicate, leggy manner, with narrow green and yellow leaves that arch over pots and macrame hangers in dainty trailing stems of white flowers and tiny new spider plants. This is a spider you won't mind joining you on your tuffet.

Spider plants truly are here to serve. They are not toxic for cats and dogs or even for humans with a taste for houseplants. They actually remove toxins, sucking in formaldehyde from your dirty indoor air.

Love your spider plant like your spider plant loves you. They are pretty chill about how much light they need. Stick with the popular houseplant "medium" light, bright and indirect. Water them well when their soil is dry—they like a fast-drying potting mix so their roots don't soak, but will need extra water in the summer months. They don't need to be repotted often because they work harder at making babies than at growing roots—who can blame them?—so move the plant to a larger pot only when the root ball starts growing through or over the pot.

Spider plants have achieved legendary status in houseplant popularity in part because they are not overwhelmingly hard to care for, but there are a few unsightly problems to avoid. It starts with the leaf tips:

Black or dark brown tips. Overwatering keeps the roots too wet to absorb nutrients. They begin to rot in a muddy pot, and that spreads into ugly black tips on those dainty leaves. Lay off the water! Wait until the top inch of soil is dry before adding more and make sure the pot is draining well—this goes for hanging pots, too.

Pale brown tips. You'll probably also spot limp, listless leaves when your plant is thirsty. Spider plants don't like to dry out between baths. Water often enough that your (well-drained) soil stays damp.

Keep an eye on your plant's roots, too. When it is outgrowing its pot, its roots will take up too much pot space to leave room for absorbent soil. Without soil to hold a little moisture near the roots at all times, it will dry out much more quickly.

Brown tips. This is a tropical plant, so it loves tropical air. A little more humidity, please! Spider plants do well with regular misting.

Gray or rusty tips. Spider plants can be a little sensitive about what kind of water you give them. If your tap water contains chemicals like chlorine and fluoride, that's good for you, but bad for your spider plant. Leave water out overnight to allow the chemicals to evaporate before watering your plant.

Overfertilizing can also put too many chemicals into your spider plant's pot. Stick to spring and summer for feeding, and if salts and chemicals are building up in the soil, water until the water flows through the drainage holes, rinsing out impurities.

Yes, that's a lot of brown in your tips. Which brown is it? Dark? Pale? Somewhere in between? If the tips are brown and the soil is soaked, you might adjust for overwatering. If the tips are brown and drooping, underwatering should be top of mind. It can vary from plant to plant, so you will have to use your judgment.

Also watch out for:

Brown leaves. Too much sun! Move out of direct light or the leaves will get burned brown.

Yellow leaves. Not enough sun! Move closer to a window to keep those leaves green.

If you care for your spider plant well, you will get spider babies! This may sound a little like bringing home a hamster from the pet store and discovering it's pregnant, but spider plant free love is nothing to be scared of and can create a whole family of houseplants to decorate your home and share with your bemused friends. The parent plant produces lovely little white flowers, which grow on trailing yellow stems; from each of these a tiny spider plantlet grows. Wait until the tiny plant starts growing aerial roots. Then clip it from the stem and pot it (or if it has yet to develop roots, let it sit in water for a few weeks and roots will grow)! Brand-new spider plant, at your service.

Staghorn Fern
Platycerium bifurcatum

Light: bright indirect light

Water: weekly in summer, less often in winter

Soil: sphagnum moss or peat, no soil

Food: monthly water-soluble solution

Pot: attach to wall mount or hanging basket

The staghorn fern gets a rep for being high-maintenance largely because you can't just shove it in a pot and dump some soil on it. It doesn't want all of that. That's not high-maintenance. It just wants it the way it wants it.

This fern is an epiphyte, growing on trees or other plants rather than in soil. Acknowledge that fact—and how different that makes it from your average houseplant—and suddenly its needs become clear. Not picky, just not into dirt.

Epiphytes make for fun display options, and the staghorn is the queen of the spectacle. Hanging baskets will work, or try a wall mount! Attach it to a plaque or a piece of driftwood and you have an antlered showpiece worthy of the finest hunting lodge without all the Bambi implications.

The staghorn fern has two distinct types of leaves or fronds. The shield fronds, starting off a fresh young green and turning brown over time, protect the roots and absorb nutrients and water. The other type of frond sticks out from this shield like a pair of . . . well, stag's horns. Bright green stag's horns.

Finding the right setting for your fern and finding the right watering schedule are the secret to successful staghorn ownership. Like most ferns, the staghorn prefers indirect bright light. That's the easy part. Getting the moisture right is the bigger accomplishment. Humidity is important, so keep it in a humid spot (in a bathroom? over a sink?) or mist it occasionally, focusing the spray on the shield fronds. Weekly, remove it from its mount and give it a good soak in the sink or a bowl for ten to twenty minutes, and then let it drip-dry before rehanging. We can't emphasize that last part enough. The plant shouldn't be dripping wet when it goes back to its display location, or else:

Brown antler fronds, starting at the base. This is an overwatered plant, suffering from root rot. Dry it out by removing it from its mount and ease off on the watering routine. By the time the leaves have turned black, the root rot is too advanced to save the plant.

Brown antler frond tips, wilting fronds. Time for a drink! Water the fern well and make sure to keep humidity levels up.

Black spots on fronds. Staghorn ferns suffer from rhizoctonia disease, caused by too much moisture. Make sure it's in a location where it gets good air circulation and hold off on watering and misting to give it a chance to heal.

Pale or browning leaf color. Ferns like indirect sun. Too much intense direct sun, especially hot afternoon sun, will give these antlers a sunburn. Move them to a bright but not sunny location.

Mealybugs and white scale. When your staghorn fern has suffered at all—whether from lack of humidity, too much watering, etc.—it is especially susceptible to mealybugs and white scale. If you spot small spots or clusters of creatures on your fronds, treat them with an insecticide right away. Some experts advise against oil-based insecticide.

There is a certain amount of trial and error in caring for a staghorn fern. It's challenging, not difficult! When you're watering, err on the side of a slightly wilted fern rather than keeping it too wet—it will recover faster from not enough water than from the consequences of too much water. Once you have carefully developed a mutually rewarding relationship with your "high-maintenance" friend, you can give it pride of place in your home. No animals were harmed in the making of this decor.

String of Pearls
Curio rowleyanus

Light: bright sun, six to eight hours a day
Water: when soil is dry
Soil: fast-draining cactus or succulent mix
Food: fertilize monthly with diluted solution in spring and summer
Pot: repot annually, fast-draining pot

String of pearls should top any list of unique houseplants. It looks like you have strung a collection of green peas on a string (it's not anything like a pea, however, as it is definitely toxic to you and to pets). As it grows, it will dangle down as much as two feet over the edge of your pot. It's easy to grow, easy to propagate, and easy to love. Would we could all say the same.

This is a succulent, and each bead is actually a thick, juicy spherical leaf—the plant's clever water storage solution. In its African homeland, it spreads out as ground cover. In your house, you can grow it in a hanging pot or cascade it down from a windowsill or shelf. It's not a forever plant—these pearls tend to last only around five years or so—but since any strand starts over as a new plant, you can count on its offspring to carry on family traditions for generations to come.

Remember your succulent rules. Water only when the soil is dry. Those round leaves are designed to reduce leaf evaporation, meaning the plant can handle a dry spell. However, round leaves also reduce the leaf area that can absorb light, so this plant can handle more sun than many of its succulent brethren. It still doesn't like that ruthless afternoon direct sun, though. You won't need a big pot; the shallow root system of the string of pearls does just fine in a smaller setting.

When it comes to communicating its concerns, it's all in the quality of the pearl:

Flattened, collapsed pearls. The water storage tanks are low. Send in the water! Water thoroughly until water drips through the drainage holes.

Burst, mushy, shriveled pearls. You have overwatered this poor succulent until its leaves have burst from excessive hydration. The soil, preferably something sandy and quick-drying like a cactus mix, should fully dry out between each watering, and a little neglect won't hurt it.

A terra-cotta or clay pot that pulls extra moisture from the soil will help keep the roots of your string of pearls from rotting. The size of the pot also matters. A pot too big for your small, shallow-rooted pearls will keep the soil damper for longer—not a good thing for a succulent. You'll also want to be thoughtful about how deeply the pearls settle into the pot. Keep the soil level high enough to ensure that they are no more than a quarter of an inch below the pot's rim. Too deep in the pot and the plant won't get adequate aeration, encouraging the damp conditions just right for root rot.

Leggy stems, scattered pearls. This plant loves light! Find it a sunny windowsill with full access to morning light (not afternoon) and at least six hours of brightness a day.

Scarred, dry pearls. We said no afternoon sun, didn't we? Those harsh, hot rays will burn the green beads brown. Those particular scars won't go away, but the plant will continue to grow if you get it out of the intense sun.

Falling pearls. When a string of pearls plant gets too chilly or its environment is too drafty (think AC vent or open window in cold weather), it can lose its pearls. Warm temperatures will keep it happy. But you're not looking to create a tropical climate. Avoid too much humidity as well.

Yellow or sooty pearls. The real curse of the black pearl is probably an aphid. String of pearls isn't particularly prone to pests, but when it's infected by aphids or mealybugs, they can leave behind a sticky substance that leads to sooty mold. When you see off-colored pearls, treat the plant with an insecticidal soap and rinse it well when you water.

Those trailing stems of green globes are just made for a lesson in easy succulent propagation. Clip off a section of stem and pearls. Let the cut end heal over for twenty-four hours. Place the strand atop some damp succulent potting mix, tucking in the stem end. No watering! Just wait two or three weeks until new roots form. Succulents grow slowly from cuttings at first, but it won't be too many more weeks before tiny new teardrop-shaped leaves begin to appear and then grow into fully formed round pearls. Now *those* are some pearls you'll be proud to clutch.

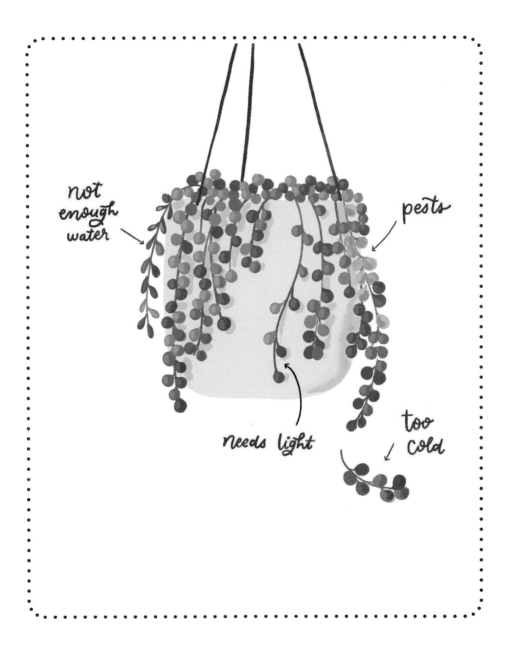

UMBRELLA PLANT

SCHEFFLERA

Light: bright indirect light
Water: weekly, when soil is dry
Soil: nutrient-rich potting mix
Food: monthly liquid fertilizer during spring and summer
Pot: repot annually, or less to control growth

Take shelter under this umbrella!

The schefflera is a lush tropical plant with a forgiving nature and easygoing needs. Called the umbrella plant after the look of its oval green leaves arching out from a central stalk, the schefflera is perfectly designed to be a houseplant.

It likes regular and thorough watering, but wants to dry out in between, so no need to constantly fuss over the right moisture level. It's happy with the indirect light that most homes provide and will grow quickly again when you prune it back from the legginess it achieves if that light is too limited. And sure, it needs misting sometimes, but doesn't that extra bit of humidity feel good for you, too?

Young umbrella plants or dwarf varietals are small enough to sit on your desk or table, while as they grow large, they can fill an entire corner with leafy greenness. To maintain your schefflera long enough for it to reach its large-houseplant potential, pay attention to the secrets it whispers under the umbrella:

Yellow, dropped leaves. The umbrella plant is easy to overwater, as you tend to think of it as a tropical plant that needs constant moisture. Actually it prefers to get a little dry between showers, so when you do water it, it needs to be properly soaked and drained thoroughly. This can be difficult with a large pot. Remember: The goal is to avoid having water pooling and sitting around the plant's soil and roots, a muddy situation that can quickly result in root rot. Dead roots equal yellow, dead leaves.

Limp, droopy leaves. Curling brown leaves. The first stage of underwatering is limp leaves. If you continue to skip watering, those lovely glossy leaves will curl and start to brown. Slake its thirst and stay consistent on watering.

Pests! The umbrella plant can be an easy target for mini houseplant invaders. Aphids—small green plant-juice feeders—leave behind a "honeydew," the nice word for aphid excrement, that leads to sooty mold. Spider mites can be spotted by their webs. Treat both and any other pests with an insecticidal soap and stave off future outbreaks by increasing humidity. A little mist keeps the pests away!

Leggy stems. Those stems are stretching long and lanky because they are trying to get better access to light. Move your plant to a brighter location. Prune back stretched-out lengths and it will grow back full and bushy.

Brown leaves. Of course, moving it into direct sun will cause more problems than it will cure. Bright light, but always indirect, to avoid sunburns.

Rootbound. Roots pushing against the edge of the pot? That's what a rootbound plant looks like. The umbrella plant doesn't mind being rootbound too much; in fact, keeping it slightly rootbound can help prevent it from growing too large. However, the pot will eventually be filled with all root, no soil, and then the plant can't absorb water well. Time to repot. Your umbrella plant may shed a few leaves from the stress of a new home, but it will recover.

As your umbrella plant ages, it will shed a few leaves along the way. They yellow, wither, and fall away. This is a normal part of aging and nothing to panic about. The yellowed and lost leaves to watch for are more ubiquitous; if a lot of leaves look unhealthy, get to work on plant health care!

There's one more way a schefflera can shuffle off its leaves, and it's not one you want to find out about the hard way: Do not let pets or small children chew on these leaves! The leaves contain calcium oxalate crystals, toxic to animals and humans. You'll start with burning and stinging in the mouth and then in the intestines, sometimes leading to long-term kidney damage. Let's just not.

Venus Flytrap

Dionaea muscipula

Light: twelve hours of direct sun

Water: rainwater or distilled water, consistently moist

Soil: Venus flytrap mix or peat moss with perlite

Food: do not fertilize

Pot: plastic or ceramic pot

It figures that a plant this creepy (a carnivorous plant? *eww*) is American made. Originating in the bogs of North and South Carolina—where it has nearly been eliminated in the wild—the venus flytrap is a houseplant of unique style and needs.

It's a petite plant, only six to twelve inches tall when fully grown. Its leaves are divided into two parts—a flat green leaf and then the culminating "trap" the plant is known for. The trap consists of two lobes hinged together, sticky pink in the center, and edged with hairlike extrusions. The first half of its name is an allusion to the trap's resemblance to a certain portion of a lady's anatomy (think Goddess of Love), and the second half references its unusual feeding habits.

The home you're trying to re-create for your venus flytrap is less New York flower shop and more Carolina swampland: damp, hot, and buggy. Water often, keeping the soil moist and using only chemical-free water. As soon as the surface soil dries, give it another drink. It wants hot direct sun. A secluded windowsill will not do—we're looking for at least twelve hours of sunbathing. This requirement may necessitate moving the plant around if your windows are in shadow part of the day.

And then there are the bugs. Venus flytraps consume flies, mosquitoes, and other bugs to get their nutrients. If it's living outside in a bog, it can feed itself. Inside, it's all on you, Seymour. Some venus flytrap aficionados insist on live bugs, usually purchased at a pet store. Others are fine with freeze-dried mealworms. Gently place the bug inside the trap, and if the bug is dead, nudge it around to make contact with the interior "hairs." That contact triggers the trap to close over the bug, which will slowly be digested and absorbed inside the plant over the next four to ten days.

Time for a little venus flytrap Q&A.

Why are the traps turning black and dying?
- Traps do not live indefinitely. Each one has a set number of times it can open and close, lasting around three months. Don't worry when one trap dies. Others will take its hungry place.
- Overfeeding is a risk for venus flytraps as well as humans! It takes a tremendous amount of plant energy to close a trap, so only feed one or two at a time to avoid the plant's overexerting itself. Similarly, too large a meal can be stressful. The bug should be no more than a third of the trap size. The trap needs to be able to fully seal closed over the bug to absorb it.
- The venus flytrap does have a dormant period in the fall and winter; it closes up shop, looks like it's dead, and survives through

its rhizomes under the soil. It'll pop back up when the sun heats up the world again.

Why is my plant sad and withered?

- **Light.** It really does need twelve sunny hours. It's not a big plant, so if you need to move it from a morning light window to an afternoon light window—well, this is the project you signed up for when you got a venus flytrap.
- **Thirst.** That damp soil is important to remind it of its boggy past. Yes, your pot needs to drain, as is true with almost all houseplants. But check the soil moisture regularly and top it off as soon as the surface is dry.
- **Chemicals.** The venus is pure. No hard-water chemicals. Use only distilled water or collected rainwater. Some pots, like terra-cotta or clay, can also leach chemicals into the soil. Use a plastic or ceramic pot. Most potting soils also have minerals and fertilizers mixed in. Use a specific venus flytrap mix, or combine peat moss and sand or perlite to make your own. No fertilizer. It gets its nutrients from its dinner.

Venus flytraps are popular gifts for kids. After all, how often do you find an interactive houseplant? This is a great lesson in responsibility and learning routines. However, don't let the young'uns poke their fingers in the traps just to watch them close. No, the flytrap doesn't feed on human blood. Yes, it does exhaust and damage the plant to move the trap unnecessarily.

WEEPING FIG

FICUS BENJAMINA

Light: bright indirect light

Water: water consistently, keeping soil moist

Soil: rich, fast-draining soil

Food: fertilize monthly, slow-release fertilizer

Pot: repot every two years

Let's start with how the weeping fig got its name. It will explain so much about its up-keep. It is called the "weeping" fig because it is so neurotically sensitive to the slightest environmental variation that caring for it may reduce you to tears.

Feeling better about any problems you may be having with your *Ficus benjamina*? It's not you, it's the fig!

Also popularly called just ficus—not to be confused with the fiddle-leaf fig (*Ficus ly-rata*) or the rubber plant (*Ficus elastica*), both covered elsewhere in this book—the leafy, branchy, daintily woodsy weeping fig is a beloved indoor gardening friend, in spite of its challenges. Like a fragile and demanding movie star, when it performs, how can you resist? Its oval green leaves arranged on woody branches give it the charm of a decidu-ous shade tree in the compact shape of an evergreen houseplant. Dedicate yourself to learning its language up front and you can enjoy a pleasantly woodland environment in your very own living room.

First, pick the perfect spot for your ficus. Be sure it is perfect, because the weep-ing fig does not like to be moved. If you're someone who likes to rearrange your furni-ture frequently, or if you see yourself moving a lot, prepare yourself for a fussy ficus, dropping leaves all over the place. Your chosen setting also needs consistent tempera-tures. Next to a heater is not a good spot. Next to an AC vent is not a good spot. Find more even temperatures and it will be happy. Growing as high as six feet indoors, it can be quite a statement houseplant, so your ficus location should be a highlight of your home.

That location needs to be near enough to a light source (or as we sometimes like to call it, a window) to get lots of bright light during the day. But we're talking about indirect light. As is true with many plants, hot sun beaming directly on green leaves will kill ficus. Too much shade, however, leads to a sad weeping fig. Keep it bright, but not intense.

The watering schedule, however, can be a little intense. This is not one of those plants that comfortably dries out between waterings. Ficus likes to be damp. Water often enough that the soil stays moist but not wet. Soaking soil around the roots will cause them to rot. Let the water drain out thoroughly after watering. The best advice is to get on a workable schedule and stick with it.

Listening to your ficus recount its grievances can be tedious, since it really has one primary choice of communication: dropping leaves. Did you move the ficus from its location? Leaf drop. Did it get a little cold during winter months? Leaf drop. Did you water too often? Leaf drop. Is it a bit shady in your place? Leaf drop. Yes, this is stressful, but focus on your ficus and you'll figure it out. Go through the checklist of weeping fig frailties:

Light. Is it bright enough? Low light is stressful for a fig.

Water. There are two potential problems with water: underwatering or overwatering. Underwatering has an easy solution. Water your dried-out plant. Water it often enough to keep the soil moist. Overwatering is easier to avoid, but harder to solve. When the soil is very wet around the roots, they cannot absorb nutrients from the soil and start to die and rot. You must have a pot that drains water away from the roots before it can collect there. And you must not water so often that the soil feels boggy. Give roots a chance to dry out for new, healthy roots to grow.

Temperature. A Goldilocks plant likes to stick to the same temperature year-round. If your home swings wildly from hot to cold and back again, a ficus is going to struggle. Weeping figs, which are tropical plants, also enjoy some humidity. Mist its leaves on occasion, or place it near/on a tray of damp pebbles for some damper air (which also helps keep the temperature consistent).

Fertilizer. Weeping figs are nutrient gobblers. While some houseplants can get by without fertilizer and maybe just need the soil refreshed, the ficus needs fertilizing. It also needs refreshed soil annually, even if you're not repotting. Scoop out the old stuff from around the root ball and add in some fresh soil. Of course the ficus will probably drop leaves when you do this!

Change in location. Sometimes you have to move a ficus. Accept that it will drop its leaves at the horrible stress of this experience and don't worry about it.

Pests. When you have eliminated all the other concerns, check leaves for aphids or spider mites! They can be wiped off or removed with an insecticide.

Most important, remember: If your ficus has dropped all of its leaves in the middle of a temperament, you don't actually need to weep. Leaves grow back.

YUCCA

Light: full sun to bright indirect light
Water: when dry, every one to two weeks
Soil: well-draining potting mix; may add sand or perlite
Food: fertilize monthly in spring and summer
Pot: repot every two to three years, or refresh soil

So many of our houseplants are imports from faraway times and places. How nice to meet a homegrown American native plant. Yuccas, in their many different varieties, proliferate in Central and South America and all over the southeastern United States.

When shopping for a new yucca plant, be aware that there are many different species. The two most often recommended for indoor growing are nicknamed spineless yucca (*Yucca gigantea,* aka *Yucca guatemalensis,* aka *Yucca elephantipes,* but what's in a name, right?) and Spanish bayonet (*Yucca aloifolia*). The difference is right there in the name: The first has softer leaves without a sharp spine. The second has stiff leaves, with a sharp needle point at the end. Both make a striking addition to your home and share common care needs, so pick according to your taste. Looking to ward off unwanted guests? Park a Spanish bayonet in your foyer. Got a small space where you may bump into a houseplant unexpectedly? Better stick with the more touchable spineless yucca.

Yucca is known for its green swordlike leaves (whether they are stiff or soft) perched atop a long, straight trunk. They are sometimes mistaken for a corn plant (*Dracaena*) but grow rather differently. As they mature, lower leaves will naturally fall off and the trunk will continue to extend.

As a dry climate native, yucca does well with neglect. Water when the soil is dry and make sure it drains well. Low humidity is just fine—you will not need or want to mist this desert friend. It would love some full sun, like a western or southern window, but indirect light works, too, as long as it is very bright for a good part of the day. You won't have to repot often, since the yucca grows slowly indoors and prefers to be a bit rootbound. That's a good thing, since a larger yucca can be hard to shift to a new pot. Sometimes it's best to just replace the old soil with fresh stuff every year or two.

When your yucca says yuck:

Yellow leaves. Be honest, have you been overwatering? If the soil is staying wet between showers, your yucca is getting too much liquid. Check also for a mushy or spongy trunk. Beneath the soil, you may well find root rot. Clear out wet, dirty soil and dead roots and give your yucca a clean, dry home. You need a pot with good drainage, and that pot should be no more than an inch larger than the root ball—larger pots stay wet longer. A watering routine is not reliable. Feel the soil before you water. Dry? You can water. Wet? Leave it alone.

Darker green leaves. If your yucca's leaves are progressively getting darker green, this can be an early sign that the plant isn't getting enough light. It's storing up as much light as possible in those leaves, but eventually they'll turn yellow, then dry brown, and eventually they will fall off if the plant remains in the shade. Low light settings can also cause a stretched-out, leggy appearance with limited leaves. Yucca is a bright light plant. Get it some sun.

Brown patches on the leaves. Moving a shade-grown plant abruptly into the hot sun, however, can give it a sunburn. Help it adjust gradually to brighter light, rather than shifting it directly into the sun. If you need to move a yucca from a shady corner, try it in a spot with bright but indirect light first. Later you can work on the direct sun location.

Wilting. You won't have to transplant a yucca often, but when you do, it may get a little nervous about the experience. Don't be surprised if it looks depressed at first. Give it a few days (don't overwater it while it adjusts) and it will be fine.

Brown leaf edges and tips, leaf drop. Yuccas don't care for fertilizer. Flush the soil with a heavy watering (but with complete drainage, too!).

Scale or other pests. Treat small brown bugs or other pests with insecticide or neem oil. They are not a huge problem for the yucca as long as it is healthy.

Yuccas can eventually, though slowly, grow quite large. If yours is starting to dominate the space, pruning back the stalks to the main trunk can keep it under control. You can even root these stalks in potting mix and start a whole new crop of yucca!

Zebra Haworthia

Haworthiopsis Attenuata

Light: bright indirect light

Water: when dry, every one to two weeks

Soil: cactus or succulent potting mix

Food: cactus fertilizer in summer months only

Pot: repot when plant and offsets are too large for the pot, four to five years

The houseplant that makes you say, "Aww." Is there any plant more adorable than the diminutive haworthia? No more than six inches high—and usually smaller—it perches in petite pots, cheery in its green and white stripes, and so remarkably undemanding that the biggest risk to its health is your helicopter plant parenting.

Small but sturdy, haworthias somewhat resemble the aloe plant—thick fleshy green leaves attenuating into points arranged in a rosette pattern. What earns the plant its "zebra" nickname is, of course, its stripes: White bands or strips of white bumps arranged across the green leaves in a striped pattern.

There are actually two brands of haworthia nicknamed "zebra." *Haworthiopsis attenuata* has stripes on both sides of its leaves, while the *Haworthia fasciata* is striped and bumpy on the outer leaf edge and smooth green on the inner edge. Both are super cute, so who cares?

Stick to the succulent rules of care for these little darlin's: water when the soil is dry, keep out of direct sun, avoid humidity, and relax. A happy haworthia will even produce a whole offset crop of baby haworthias along its base. When these spread enough to take over the surface of the pot, separate them into new pots of their own and give your original zebra plant some fresh soil. It's worked hard to keep you in haworthia heaven.

What to do when a cutie-pie gets mad at you:

Yellow, mushy leaves. This is the big key to succulent care: do not overwater. A succulent sitting in wet soil will never survive. Water only when the soil is dry. A big problem for cute plants is the regrettable tendency to house them in cute containers. Yes, that teacup or tiny bowl is charming. No, it is not a good succulent container if it doesn't have drainage holes. Drill holes in the bottom of the container or get rid of it. A succulent sitting in wet soil will rot. Once the center rosette is mushy, it is nearly impossible to save, so avoid dampness altogether.

When you water, aim for the roots. Keep water out of the center of the rosette, where it will produce just the humid, soggy conditions that inspire rotten haworthias.

Puckered, withered leaves. This is a tough one. If the soil is dry, your little zebra may need water. If it plumps up again after a bath, then it's fine. If the soil is wet, withered leaves can be an indicator of root rot.

Changing leaf color. In their South African homeland, zebra plants tuck themselves under the shadow of a rock or tree to hide from excessive sun exposure. Leaves that turn red or purple or brown are getting too much direct sun. Leaves that turn white are sunburned. Shift to the shade.

healthy   too much   too much
               water   sun

Pale green, leggy leaves. Still desert plants, haworthias do need brightness. When the color fades to light green and those attenuate leaves stretch out or spread out even more, get them a brighter location.

Collapsed center. Haworthias like to breathe. Good air circulation is important, so don't tuck them in a stagnant corner. If there's a fan or a draft in the area, they'll be happier and less likely to develop the humidity-induced rot that will cause the center of the rosette to yellow and fall in on itself.

Mealybugs. While pests are not common for these arid houseplants, if they do infect your zebra plant, wipe them away with a cotton swab dipped in rubbing alcohol.

To sum up: easy care, cunning appearance, and those interesting bumpy zebra stripes. Is a home complete without a haworthia?

ZZ Plant

Zamioculcas zamiifolia

Light:	bright indirect light
Water:	when dry, every one to two weeks
Soil:	well-draining potting mix
Food:	fertilize with diluted solution once during growing season
Pot:	repot when rhizomes push through soil

Zamioculcas zamiifolia—try saying that five times fast. No wonder this houseplant sticks with its nickname, ZZ plant.

With this plant's shiny zigzag leaves, its patience for your neglect and general ineptitude, and its reputation for removing air toxins from any space it inhabits, we really can't understand why this is a popular fake plant style. Just get the real thing, the one and only ZZ!

ZZ plant, also known as the Zanzibar gem, hails from Africa, where it has been accustomed to some dry spells and has adapted to store water in big chunky rhizomes that look like potatoes nestled in the soil. With this storage system, it wants you to forget to water! Let the soil completely dry out and then water thoroughly, pouring in enough water to flow freely through the soil and out the drainage holes. This will ensure that your plant is wet, the soil is wet, and the excess water has washed away any soil or fertilizer impurities. Now just wait for it to dry out again and check in a couple of weeks.

No direct sunlight, but ZZ starts looking scraggly when it doesn't get enough light. Go with a medium level of exposure or lots of "unnatural" light from lamps and indoor lights. Also, those polished leaves will need regular dusting to keep sucking in that light!

When the ZZ loses its za za zu:

Yellow leaves. Like most plants that are drought tolerant, the ZZ plant is not flood tolerant. Overwatering, keeping the soil constantly damp and soggy around the rhizomes, will cause them to rot, and that will kill a plant quickly. When whole stems full of leaves turn yellow, it's time for a rescue. Repot, getting rid of muddy soil and removing any rotten rhizomes and roots. Let it dry out well in its fresh clean soil and pot—and in the future, hold off on the wet stuff.

Brown edges, limp, drooping leaves. Neglect is one thing. Never watering is another, and eventually even the patient ZZ plant will start to wilt from lack of moisture. Keep an eye on how long it takes for the soil to dry and then stick to an appropriate watering schedule. You will need to adjust the schedule in colder, darker months, when water evaporates more slowly.

Brown-edged leaves can also be a complaint about a lack of humidity. If you live in an especially dry area, place a tray of damp pebbles near your plant or add an occasional misting to your ZZ routine.

all yellow leaves =
overwatered

brown edges, drooping leaves =
needs water

yellow spots or streaks =
too much direct sun

brown leaves =
chemical buildup in soil

Brown leaves. ZZ plants can be sensitive to chemical buildup in their soil. That's why we advise thoroughly watering each time, as it rinses away fertilizer, salts, and hard-water chemicals that collect in the soil over time.

Leggy stems. Big gaps between leaves, like a first-grader's front teeth? ZZ needs a little light! Indirect light is great, but it still needs at least six hours of bright light a day.

Yellow or brown patches on leaves. Direct light, however, will burn even the hardiest of ZZ plants. Keep it away from intense sun to avoid the sunburned look. Sunburned leaves will not turn green again, so consider removing them for a prettier plant. Just don't remove all the leaves at once!

Yellow patches and spots on leaves. Even the best of plants can fall prey to a bad influence, like a gang of spider mites. The healthier your plant is, the less likely it will be victimized, but if you fall off your watering routine, spider mites and other bugs can move in. Remove them with insecticide and protect your plant's overall health in the future to avoid them.

Roots pushing through the soil and even the pot. Rhizomes will grow as your plant grows! Eventually they'll get too big to be contained. Time to repot.

Be good to your ZZ plant and it will be good to you. It's on the NASA list of air-purifying plants, with a talent for removing toxins like xylene, toluene, and benzene from the air. Beautiful and talented. How can you resist?

CONCLUSION

Yes, plant parenting can have its challenges.

No, you should not let worries about the difference between *root rot* and *rootbound* scare you away from the joys of sharing your home with a houseplant.

Instead, take the guidance on potential problems plants present as an opportunity to identify the perfect plant for your personality. Welcome to your plant therapy session.

Are you someone who's on the road a lot, who never plans, who never tries the same thing twice, who may remember a friend's birthday, but also may not? You're not distant, uncommitted, or indifferent. You're a free spirit, a joyful energy that can't be tied down by rules and schedules. In fact, you're just perfect for a similarly unscheduled plant, one that thrives in inconsistent conditions and enjoys a little space in a relationship themselves. You're a ZZ plant parent. You'd also be the beloved of a pothos or a spider plant. Even some succulents and cacti would do well with the kind of on-again, off-again attention you're prepared to give. And then of course there's the obvious match for the most capricious of indoor gardeners: a cast iron plant.

Or perhaps you're one of those unrelentingly involved types, constantly wanting to talk about the relationship, present in every moment, hovering over every move. You're not a helicopter, codependent, or interfering. You're a nurturer! A fern would just love you. It would revel in your steadfast attention to its soil moisture levels and love the way you treat it to regular humidity. A ficus or fiddle-leaf fig, too, would enjoy your devotion. You would always be there, sympathetic to why it didn't like to be moved or how uncomfortable dim light made it.

See? All you needed was a little self-awareness and a comprehensive book on plant problems to find your perfect match.

A successful plant/person relationship is symbiotic. You have now learned the keys to making sure your contributions to the partnership are positive ones. But this isn't a one-way street. Your houseplant is here to help you as well.

You may or may not remember your high school science class explanations of plant respiration, so here's the simple version. While humans breathe in oxygen and breathe out carbon dioxide, plants absorb carbon dioxide and produce oxygen. Further, plants actually help filter dangerous toxins from the air in enclosed areas. Their respiration process removes many common "sick building" by-products of cleaning materials, paint, and plastics (like formaldehyde or ammonia) from the atmosphere around them, turning any space they occupy into a better place to inhale.

Take a deep breath and thank your houseplant.

Feeling more relaxed? Of course you are! Because houseplants have been shown to reduce stress. Hospital patients with green plants in their surroundings instead of just sickly green wall paint have a faster recovery time. Offices with plant decor are sites of greater worker happiness. If just looking at plants helps soothe your brain, imagine how it feels spending time gardening. Putting your hands in the dirt, messing around with water, pruning, potting—these may sound like chores, but the simple act of maintaining plants can lower your stress level.

Once your stress is eased, your brain has room to focus on other opportunities. Several studies have demonstrated greater productivity when people share their space with plants. Those offices that had happier workers because of their indoor plants also had more productive workers. Children in school classrooms that include plants have higher test scores. Something in our perception of plant life stimulates our brains to do better.

With all these wonderful gifts plants bring to your partnership, your own tasks of keeping organized on water and finding a nice pot seem pretty easy.

Like your human relationships (you *do* talk to someone besides a houseplant, right?), while each plant/person relationship has elements in common with others, each one is also unique. Many of the plants profiled in these pages, have dozens to hundreds of varietals. As branches of one genus, their needs may be similar, but they may require some small tweaks to align their care. A more variegated leaf, for example, will require more light than a predominantly green one. Your unique environment, too, can require a few changes to standard plant care advice. If you live in an extremely dry environment, lack of humidity becomes an important focus if you're dedicated to raising a tropical plant. Be ready with your tray of wet pebbles. A very wet climate, on the other hand, may mean you need to be especially watchful that soil dries out well between waterings for your plants that prefer arid conditions.

Learning your plant's special wants and habits is both a challenge and a reward. It's all about good communication. Listen carefully—what is your plant telling you?

Acknowledgments

Writers, like houseplants, need a lot of care, patience, and sunshine. I am grateful to all those who have kindly nurtured me in this process:

Loni Harris, whose brilliant artwork brings this book to life.

Crystal Desilet of Cactus Moon Market (cactusmoonmarket.com) for her expertise on succulents and all things houseplant.

Hannah Robinson, Samantha Lubash, and the Simon Element team for this wonderful opportunity to bring a little plant life into the world.

Emily Sylvan Kim and Ellen Brescia of et al Creative for their encouragement, sympathy, humor, insight, and so many other enthusiastic adjectives.

And of course, to my family, who have made space for so many houseplants in our life.

Index

About the Author

Emily L. Hay Hinsdale is a freelance writer, an enthusiastic cook, a dedicated traveler, a determined pedestrian, and a lifelong gardener.

About the Illustrator

Loni Harris specializes in hand-lettering and florals and has had artwork with major U.S. retailers such as Walmart, Target, Home Depot, and Staples. She loves hiking, working on her farm, and binge-watching while sketching.